A Century
in the Garden

A Century
in the Garden

One Hundred Years at
Kelley & Kelley Nursery

Steve Kelley

NODIN PRESS

Design: John Toren
Composed in Galliard and Charcuterie Contrast

9 8 7 6 5 4 3 2 1

ISBN: 978-1-947237-40-7
Library of Congress Control Number: 2022933636

Published by
Nodin Press
5114 Cedar Lake Road,
Minneapolis, MN 55416
www.nodinpress.com

Printed in USA

To the generations of Kelleys before me
who so capably set the stage at Kelley & Kelley,
allowing my role to be so joyously played,
and to Arla, who makes me smile.

APPRECIATION

If, like me, you enjoy reading the appreciation page even before delving into the book, let me introduce you to the three people integral to the publication of these essays. First, Cindy Jamison. Persistent Cindy. Cindy coaxed me—nay, admonished me—time and again over the years to put these ramblings into book form, until one day she showed up on my doorstep, publisher in one hand and a tray of coffee in the other. That was that. Thank you, Cindy. Then there is said publisher, Norton Stillman of Nodin Press. This fellow could charm the birds out of the trees. Who could say no to Norton? Persistent Norton. Over several years he cajoled me along, "How's the book coming, Steve?" Thank you, Norton. Of course, a book has to have an editor; Norton introduced me to John Toren. I thought my words suited me just fine, but John proved me wrong in more than one instance. He skillfully smoothed my sentences into lyric form and gently but firmly kept me on schedule. Semi-persistent John. Thank you John.

Contents

A Century
in the Garden

My Early Years

My name is Steve Kelley, I was born in 1947 and have lived in Long Lake—barely a mile from my childhood home as the crow flies—all my life. I have three brothers, we all got along well growing up, and get along well still. Mom kept busy doing everything moms did in the fifties and sixties and seventies to raise the family and keep the household running smoothly, for which she was rightly proud and for which she was well regarded in the close-knit local community. Dad was at the helm of Kelley & Kelley and very civic-minded, serving terms on the school board and park board. They're both gone now.

A creek, often dry in the summer, meandered through a wooded ravine behind our house, and there were hills and fields and swamps, all splendid spots for kids to explore. There were always lots of friends around. No trouble keeping busy, summer and winter. We didn't know the meaning of boredom; Mom certainly saw to that. An especially tall old spruce tree in the side yard had branches nicely spaced for climbing. A vantage point from one of the highest branches, to which we'd nailed a small piece of wood for a seat, afforded great vistas in all directions. Up there, I could spy on the neighbors for hours or, being a dreamy kid, just sit and track the clouds floating by. We always had animals—mostly dogs—but I seem to remember chickens as well, though my brothers all accuse me of having a faulty memory. Maybe it was just those little pastel-colored chicks that came at Easter time.

There was a milkman who came twice a week. His provisions were chilled with blocks of ice (boy, I'm really making myself feel ancient) and I enjoyed trailing the water that dripped from the truck as he came and went. We burned the garbage out back in a fifty-five-gallon drum, clothes were hung on a clothes line strung between two elm trees and a telephone pole (do you think the younger generation knows why telephone poles are called telephone poles?) and we dressed up on Sunday afternoons to visit aunts and uncles in Richfield and Crystal—jaunts that today take minutes, but back then seemed akin to Lewis and Clark expeditions. Grandmother and Grandfather (on my dad's side) lived next door, so we boys felt spoiled from the start. Both Grandmother and Mom were stellar in the kitchen, and I think they kind of vied for honors in the cookie and pie department. Mom

would have been crushed to hear me say it, but I liked Grandmother's pie crust better. I suspect it was the lard.

A large garden—and I mean large—provided all manner of vegetables and fruits. The freezer and the rows of shelves in the basement could always be counted on to provide the fixings for nutritious meals. Green Giant (or the Pillsbury Doughboy, for that matter) was hardly a known entity in our house.

I attended third grade at that small schoolhouse at the corner of Watertown Road and Stubbs Bay Road. My teacher was Mrs. Dettloff, who was a favorite. Didn't every youngster have a crush on the third grade teacher? That fall, I thought Mrs. Dettloff might appreciate a gift of some of those orangey leaves I'd collected from the plants that grew in tight groups along the banks of the creek. Wouldn't she be impressed with my thoughtfulness! Mom came in as I was sorting through the pile of leaves on my bed—I wanted just the best ones for my dear teacher—and was somewhat horrified to discover that I was learning about poison ivy the hard way. It's a good thing those leaves didn't go any further than my room; Mrs. Dettloff surely would have been mighty unhappy with Steve Kelley. Boy, have I been an ace at indentifying poison ivy ever since.

A trail connected our yard with the Kelley & Kelley property, passing through yet another ravine and creek, more woods, and a farm field before reaching what to me was a wondrous place: my great grandparents' homestead, which they settled on in the early 1900s and later turned into a nursery. Regrettably, they were gone before I got a chance to meet them, but from what I hear, the great grand-folks were dear people. They raised eight children, one of whom died at an early age from eating green apples, or so we were told. I think that was just a ploy to keep us, for whatever reason, from eating green apples ourselves. Two of the younger boys, Rod and Bill, joined together as the original Kelleys of Kelley & Kelley, making me the fourth generation Kelley here on the old home place.

Helping out summers at the nursery, I never felt it was something that I'd want to make a life's work; journalism struck me as an honorable and exciting profession. The first-rate journalism school at the University of Minnesota attracted my attention, and I thought I was on a path toward a satisfying career. The professors saw to it that I was enthused over writing and I graduated ready to make my mark. And maybe I could have, if attractive job possibilities had presented themselves. But I hated job hunting—selling myself.

The summer gave way to fall, winter, and then spring. Nothing. Dad was at the helm of Kelley & Kelley at the time and, I suspect, was feeling sorry for his son. He proposed that I sign on as a landscaping crew member for the season, with the notion that I could pick up the job search again in the fall. He paired me up with Great Uncle Rod, a landscape designer who, with his land surveyor brother, Bill, had founded the little family enterprise back in 1922. Rod took me under his wing, introducing me to clients and to what I soon enough found to be very satisfying work. Indeed, I began to see a future for myself in the family business. Rod was well-regarded by his long-time clients, who relied on his vision and expertise. In the beginning, I had neither. Was I just imagining it, or did customers back then raise their eyebrows, wondering whether this kid knew a thing or two? But I took to the work and Kelley & Kelley provided me with excellent and patient mentors. With new-found skills, I was soon enough let loose with a few customers of my own, and I fell head over heels for the work. But the thought of leaving writing behind entirely didn't suit me. I made time to set pen to paper, fashioning articles for local gardening magazines and plant society newsletters.

In a family-run business, it's common for each generation to put its own little touch on things. For me, that meant doing a better job of educating our customers, clearer signage, classes, and tours of the gardens. These were easily and inexpensively implemented, but I also wanted to do writing of some sort on behalf of Kelley & Kelley. Dad was a very frugal businessman, however, and I knew printing and mailing a company newsletter would have to wait. When Dad died in February 1992 we all mourned, but at the risk of coming off as unfeeling, I also saw the event as an opportunity to forge ahead with my publishing venture. I'd envisioned it less as an advertising tool than as an educational newsletter devoted to the same kinds of practical information and gardening wisdom that I imparted to clients who visited the nursery.

> "I enjoy everything about gardening, look forward to each day, and count myself lucky to have a spouse who feels just the same."

I had lots of ideas and was eager to get going with our little newsletter, which we dubbed *In the Garden*. I wanted the inaugural issue to be mailed in time to announce our spring open house on Mother's Day weekend, so we had to put our noses to the "ground"stone.

That first number was a slim eight pages and consisted of four rather frail articles. On the first page I described my motives in the following terms:

> *Heaven knows there are enough chores around the nursery that go unaccomplished as is. It just seemed as though we needed a means of more efficiently communicating our enthusiasms and prejudices to you. We'd love nothing more than to spend unlimited time with each of our customers in the spring and throughout the summer, but this is rarely possible. There certainly is no substitute for that personal attention, but perhaps this little newsletter can help bridge the gap a bit.*

For decades, all went along swimmingly in the writing and publishing department at Kelley & Kelley. My wife, Arla, and I yearly took the first few weeks of January to bat around ideas for articles, always wondering and worrying how yet another newsletter could possibly be fleshed out. But once ideas were agreed upon, the writing part seemed to flow without much care.

'Round about 2012, after twenty years' worth of *In the Garden*, recipients began pestering me with suggestions that the best of our gardening pieces should be published as a book. I laughed off such a notion. Did the Twin Cities need another gardening book? Finally, when friend Cindy called to announce she was bringing over a publisher I should meet, I began to come around. I was cornered. And thus, a book.

A Few Things I Know
(family history)

I suspect that this tale should begin with my great, great grandparents, Mary Shannon and Samuel Greenberry Kelley, who came up from Iowa and bought the chunk of land that in time became the homegrounds of Kelley & Kelley. I am bringing this up now because 2022 marks the one hundreth year for Kelley & Kelley—quite a landmark, I think. The Kelleys arrived here in 1903 and were soon followed by their son William Shannon and daughter-in-law Ella Virginia. The younger Kelleys came from Missouri with their seven children (another would be born later) and settled in the house owned by Will's folks. The house was a simple, white, wooden farmhouse, typical of the era, and stood on the corner of what would become K & K's woodland garden. Surrounded by grand old elms, the house's small, dark rooms were always cool in summer. I don't recall visiting in the winter, but I imagine the thinly insulated house was quite drafty then. Outside the back door, which was the one most often used, was a cast iron bell on a post alongside an ancient lilac bush which still blooms faithfully every spring in a rich shade of deep purple.

Families seemed closer back then, and I understand that the home was awash with family visitors all summer—Kelley brothers and sisters and their children, and cousins and friends of Mary and Samuel. And when Kelley & Kelley was up and running the family home even served as a bed and breakfast for an employee or two. A joyous place, but also a lot of work for Great Grandmother cooking for and attending to whoever crossed the threshold.

I remember Will (from pictures) as a dapper gent who, with his neatly clipped Vandyke beard and crisply tailored suits, struck an impressive figure astride his horse, Monte, but he was a hard worker in his day as well. He had to make ends meet and at that they often didn't. The property was a working farm (the barn and machine shed still stand) with animals of all descriptions. Cows needed milking, horses needed tending, hay needed to be put up, and a large vegetable garden needed to be looked after; it produced enough that Will took surplus into the Minneapolis farmer's market. An apple orchard on the hill south of the house required a lot of work as well. Son Bill told of being farmed out to live with a local family to work, as it was difficult to feed all the children at home.

Amidst all that, there were still flower gardens. Peonies and hardy roses still exist from that era, as does a long, low stone wall that bordered an extensive perennial garden.

After the family dispersed (four of the children staying in the Long Lake area, three moving far away) and Will and Ella died (in 1947 and 1957, respectively) the house was rented out for a while; the seasons took

The Kelley and Kelley office circa 1935

their toll, and the house was torn down in the 1960s. Incidentally, if you're paying attention and are doing the math on those children and think there should have been eight, you're right. Young Lester Kelley, in his teens, died a year after the family settled in Long Lake of a ruptured appendix, though as kids we were told the cause was eating green apples.

When we began the painful process in the 1980s of removing diseased elms from around the home site, we found them to be well over 130 years old, so they existed long before the Kelleys arrived on the scene. The trees sheltered a fine grass lawn that extended north from the house 125 feet to Watertown Road. I well remember picnics and games on that magnificently-shaded expanse of lawn. The dappled shade was a splendid feature of the property. One tree that does still exist from the early days is likely well over 150 years old. It's the scraggly old boxelder south of the greenhouse. I climbed in it as a kid and Rod had

19

similar memories of his childhood. Most of the other trees on the property—birch, spruce, arborvitae, ginkgo, locust and maple—remain from the time that nursery stock was planted, some of it using horse and wagon, by Will and son Lloyd. But I'm getting ahead of the tale.

In 1922 two of Will and Ella's children, Bill (born 1893) and Rod (born 1896), joined forces and opened up shop on the home grounds as Kelley & Kelley. Rod was a landscape designer, having taken classes at both the University of Minnesota and at what is now the University of Massachusetts at Amherst. Bill received a degree in civil engineering from the University of Minnesota and practiced as a registered land surveyor. Eager and hard-working, their first office was constructed on Watertown Road just east of the family home. This small space, part of our present establishment, hints at the boys' optimism and frugality. Though times weren't the best economically speaking, still the area around Lake Minnetonka was prospering, offering the brothers a wealth of opportunity to serve the lake estates and summer homes of families from "in town." In the boys' favor as well were the facts that there wasn't a great deal of competition and they could depend on a supportive family to help get them on their feet.

Bill and Rod were quite opposites in temperament, which didn't seem at all a handicap. They both shared a positive, "make it happen" attitude, which obviously carried the day. Bill was precise, meticulous—"Put that tool, cleaned, back where you can find it in the morning"—and could be demanding. He knew the right way to do things and, by golly, that's how they would be done. He was active in county, state, and national land surveying organizations, receiving many awards for his service. On the state level, he helped establish testing requirements necessary for registration. Nationally, his work included writing a syllabus for land surveyor training. He was an accomplished wood carver, was active in Boy Scout leadership roles, and enjoyed golf, bowling, and attending U of M football games.

Rod was easy-going, creative, and the life of the party. He sought opinions and feedback ("What should we plant alongside this hosta to show it off to good effect?"). He attended the one-room log schoolhouse just east of the family homestead that was later converted into a home and much remodeled by Earl and Patty Plant. Rod was one of the founding members of St. Martin's by the Lake Church in Minnetonka Beach. He designed the pioneering fragrance garden at Camp Courage in Annandale and volunteered many hours at the camp. He had a great love for native

Bill and Rod Kelley

woodland flowers and championed their use, collecting them from local habitats before such a thing was frowned upon. In the 1960s he installed an extensive woodland garden under those old elms shading the Kelley family's front lawn when grass no longer prospered there. He was quite wicked on the tennis court in younger years, and with his wife, Marian, enjoyed collecting American antiques.

Estates were extensively landscaped back then, with long, tree-lined driveways, formal gardens, rock gardens, cutting gardens, and orchards. All this required planning, planting, and maintenance, often much more work than the estate's caretaking staff could routinely handle. Make no mistake though, it was the caretaker who ran the show. The landscape crew rarely dealt with the homeowner. Some of the caretakers could be pretty hard to please, understandably so, but if Kelley & Kelley wanted to be called back for future work it was in the landscaper's best interest to remain in the good graces of the caretaker. Sometimes this meant a little gift or two for the caretaker every now and again.

On occasion the gift-giving flowed in the opposite direction. I recall tales of one job in particular in the 1950s. A major landscaping job for a tony old folks home (as they were called then) in town kept the crew on-site for weeks at a time. Soon the management got to know the fellows and evidently appreciated their hard work, as the boys more than once were showered with gifts of food. Big wheels of imported cheese in fancy wooden boxes, slabs of well-cured ham, and baskets of the freshest of fruit all found their way back to Long Lake and—I hope—were shared with fellow workers.

Need I say that jobs in the 20s and 30s relied, in the main, on good hard labor? No labor-saving machinery back then. Horsepower was just that—horse power. If you were in landscaping you grew your own nursery stock, as did the Kelleys. This operation required nothing but work. When trees were sold for jobs, they were dug by hand, the earth ball wrapped in burlap, secured with stout twine and nails, winched onto a two-wheeled trailer, and transported to the jobsite. Ten and eleven hour days weren't uncommon. As today, the work was seasonal. Both Bill and Rod sought work in other parts of the country during the winter.

One would think that the archives of a one-hundred-year-old firm would be bursting at the seams, ripe with all sorts of bits and pieces anxious to tell tales year by year. Unfortunately that's not the case. I can't speak for Bill and Rod, but I know my dad every so often got into fits of housecleaning, and I'm sure that if dumpsters had been invented back then, he could easily have filled several at a time with stuff he considered useless that was cluttering the storage rooms at the nursery. Even so, somehow several marvelous ledgers from the mid 1920s were spared and present a picture worth re-telling. Payroll records show Bill, Rod, their brothers Lloyd, Ken, and Harold, and every so often Will with a team of horses, and local boys Guy and Lloyd Snoke with their teams as sole employees.

Rod and Bill paid themselves at the rate of 90 cents an hour, other employees received 75 cents an hour and an additional 30 cents if they supplied a team of horses. Even given the boys' penchant for squeezing every penny twice(ledgers indicate that in September of 1926 they charged their own mother $1.25 for apples from the family orchard), red ink seemed more prevalent than black in those early days. July of 1926 showed a deficit of $109.75 on sales of $1002.73, yet there was somehow $1.80 to spare for such a luxury as candy, duly and neatly set down in the ledger between a maple tree for $1.00 and two fuses for 20 cents. By spring of 1928 business had picked up enough to take on eight employees from outside the family. The area was still farm country, so I'm sure there was no lack of good, strong men willing to lend a hand. Appearing over the years on payroll records are family names such as Talbert, Nelson, Hentschel, Snoke, Dickey, Ernst, Redpath, St. John, Hallson, Neddermeyer, and Ahlstrom. Oh my, those Ahlstroms! Andy Ahlstrom was a very early employee and one of those who boarded with the Kelleys. He and his brothers (whose first names all began with the letter A, as in Adolph, Albert, Arvid, and Axel, except for John, don't ask) worked for K & K at one time or another and were good, sturdy, easygoing fellows and long-time employees.

An important and rewarding aspect of this business has been the ties to so many local families that have remained strong over the decades. Though we've worked for some pretty great families it's not my style to toss around names indiscriminately. However, in recalling customers whose landscaping projects I've been involved with over the past forty years or so, two names jumped out, begging for a word or two on this occasion.

The story is of two women of a certain age, both savvy gardeners and plantswomen. One loved nothing more than to be out with us supervising our work—in a nice way, mind you, not hovering—and the other was content to trust her gardens to our judgment. Let's call the first woman Mrs. Sumner Young and the second Marian Nellermoe. They're both gone now, sadly. I had great admiration for them and I suspect their descendants wouldn't mind my gentle remembrance.

Mrs. Y. and Mrs. N. lived on spacious properties on the other side of the lake, barely a mile from one another, and were the best of friends. They were both risk-takers, innovative, and I would say ahead of their time in the garden. At Mrs. Young's place was the first boxwood hedge—flawlessly maintained—that I'd seen around the lake. She pampered a formal bed of hybrid tea roses and provided for, at great effort (they aren't hardy and the bulbs had to be lifted and stored in the fall), a multitude of Peruvian daffodils. Garden parties should have been planned to appreciate them in bloom; they were that delightful. And asparagus. On a sunny, level part of the property, where once great beds were given over to growing vegetables and cutting flowers, only a large asparagus bed remained. It must have been half the size of our greenhouse, only a slight exaggeration. I'm hungry for asparagus just thinking of the prospect.

Down the lane at Mrs. Nellermoe's, her woodland garden on a rather steep slope south of the house was the main attraction. She and Rod were chums, and I think he could sell her on most any notion, so gradually the woodland garden expanded to a hill on the other side of the house along the driveway. These gardens were especially stunning in spring, with vast stands of maidenhair fern, Solomon's seal, bloodroot, Virginia bluebells, and trillium. The show stoppers were great clumps of both yellow and showy lady slippers. Those would have rated a garden party in their honor.

As I mentioned, these women delighted in each others' company. I will tell you, though, that they became quite competitive at one time during the gardening year: in the fall, when their orders for lily bulbs were placed. Lilies were more of a specialty item back in the 1970s. Not many gardeners then made quite the deal out of lilies as did these two women. They really were pioneers. Somehow, a rivalry developed between them over growing lilies. When the lilies were abloom, you can believe all eyes were on the Young and Nellermoe gardens. Points were given for quality and to some degree quantity of lily bloom, and also for success in growing varieties that were newish or on the marginally hardy side of things, or just generally tricky. We, of course, had to be neutral in these affairs, so no fair revealing to Mrs. Y. what Mrs. N. was ordering that season and vice-versa. You can imagine the spot this put us in. If a lily we'd planted in either garden didn't perform up to expectations or—even worse—didn't live through the winter, the consequences were felt at K & K. The lily wars went on for some years until, I guess, the point had been made that both ladies were capable of splendid displays of lilies. And perhaps that was the goal all along—to do the best, and don't fret about the competition. Life isn't a contest.

Edmund (Eddie) Phelps was a well-regarded landscape architect who developed quite a following in the area at the same time Rod & Bill were getting their feet wet. They had a congenial relationship with Mr. Phelps and implemented many of his designs. It's a delight seeing the bones of some of these early landscapes still around, considering their transitory nature. Mr. Phelps was noted for working out all the details, of recognizing the importance of getting it right from the start. This was borne out some years ago when we were reworking a formal garden he designed. This involved dividing daylilies and peonies and spading in some organic material to fluff up the soil. In our digging we came upon a system of drain tile covered with fine gravel, very obviously from Mr. Phelps' era. I'm not sure we'd take the time or make the effort to design and install such a thing these days.

A sizable job for the company in the mid-1930s was helping to landscape the George Nelson Dayton Boulder Bridge Farm on Smithtown Bay. Rock gardens were in favor at the time and Rod & Bill's younger brother Ken seemed to have an eye for their design. Nothing to it, he claimed in jest. He used to boast that he'd merely stomp around and kick a few rocks into place and there you were. We know otherwise, of course. He wasn't that magical.

For the Boulder Bridge project, weathered sandstone rocks were gathered from farm fields west of Shakopee, free for the taking. (Farmers are more savvy these days.) Near the lagoon off Smithtown Bay a pond was dug and lined with blue clay. Rocks were artfully placed, native plants were incorporated into the scheme, water was piped to cascade over the rocks, and the whole affair ended up looking pretty convincing. Last I looked, the rock work was still in place.

Bill and Rod were both avid about tennis, so it seemed natural that the firm would take up the installation of tennis courts. Har-Tru, a fine, green, granular mineral that packed firm when wet, was a product fairly new to the Midwest in the 1920s. It quickly developed quite a following as a tennis court surface hereabouts. It was quick drying, unlike impervious court surfaces, which allowed play to recommence almost immediately after rains. And a Har-Tru court also had some spring to it, making it kind to the players' knees. The old folks liked that. Tennis was an activity that people of all ages could take up, and to have one's own court at home wasn't that uncommon around the lake. Kelley & Kelley made quite a little business of installing and maintaining Har-Tru courts from the mid-1920s well up into the 1970s.

Har-Tru arrived by railcar from Hagerstown, Maryland, packaged in eighty-pound paper bags. As it took quite a number of bags of the stuff to construct a court from scratch, and several dozen bags to dress up a court in spring prior to the season, the back-breaking job of unloading Har-Tru was not one that anyone looked forward to. Those were the days before forklifts or any other sort of mechanical labor savers, so the arrival of that boxcar on a siding in Long Lake (yes, trains did stop in Long Lake, and not that long ago) was not something that we, who were low on the totem pole, anticipated with relish.

Bill oversaw the tennis court crews and he ran a tight ship. He knew all the tricks for getting soft spots or low spots in the court worked out, for setting and securing the tapes that marked the court, and for brushing and rolling to produce a surface that rated a thumbs up. We installed Har-Tru courts at all the local country clubs while also offering our services to many a private court around the lake. The rush was on in April of every year to get all the courts under our supervision up and running before the first warm days of spring. Of course, everyone wanted to be at the top of the list. Human nature.

Physically, Kelley & Kelley has grown quite a bit from the small one-room office where it started. We added a glass greenhouse in 1937 and a remodeled office and greenhouse-root cellar-garage in 1963. Nursery stock was grown in fields here until the late 1960s when that portion of the property was sold to a developer.

Changes over the years, most for the good of course, have been pretty dramatic. The use of machinery has made work less laborious. But that's been a double-edged sword. On the one hand, many a landscaper's back has been spared by the use of that forklift, but the use of the gas-engine powered device has also robbed younger generations of the advantage of knowing how to work a spade, rake, broom, or hoe. And frankly, I miss the quiet that comes courtesy of those common old tools.

The way plants are grown and shipped has magnified the gardener's options enormously. The expense and the prospect of flying plants in from the coast—or from across the globe, for that matter—wouldn't have been considered several decades ago. Now? A piece of cake. Nursery folk are no longer limited to offering their customers only locally-grown plants.

Not that many years ago, in my lifetime certainly, we were content to stock the same six hosta or handful of daylily varieties season after season. No one com-

29

plained. Now, breeding efforts have expanded offerings to the point that we're aswarm with coneflowers, coralbells, astilbes, and petunias. The wonder of tissue culture propagation has made even recently introduced plants readily available and affordable.

Used to be, the customer looking to plant a tree could expect, depending on the weather, to accomplish the job during a few weeks in spring and again in the fall when trees were dormant and could be dug. Now, trees are available for planting spring through fall, courtesy of pot-grown trees and tree spades that make child's

"When K & K began, soil was likely dug from a pit in some back corner of the nursery property. Now geraniums can luxuriate in a soil formulated just for them."

play out of digging whole fields of trees. Garden centers these days rely more on wholesale growers and less on their own production to stock their sales yards.

The use of pots has revolutionized more than just tree production. The nursery business in general couldn't have advanced to its present-day efficiency without the invention of plastic and the plastic pot. I well remember using tarpaper, papier-mâché, and even tin pots around the nursery. All were nasty, mainly because they had a tendency to stick together, and it required some force—usually beating with a shovel handle—to pry them apart. In the greenhouse, a good share of the crop was potted in clay. Though they were heavy, I still miss using clay pots to the extent we did in the past.

And soil. Did we pay as much attention to soils for potting up plants back then? I think it was pretty much one-size-fits-all. When K & K first began, soil was likely dug from a pit in some back corner of the nursery property. Now geraniums can luxuriate in a soil formulated just for them. Ditto succulents, mums, vegetables, and acid-loving plants. Nowadays soils (dirt, if you will) aren't even part of the equation. Those bags of potting soil you bring home from the garden center know nothing about dirt. It's all peatmoss, decomposed bark, perlite, and likely a bit of fertilizer. Research is constantly promoting new ideas in growing mixes and fertilizers.

Ever-changing methods of communication have revolutionized the way we learn about plants. The community of plant people who buzz and blog and twitter helps keep the latest news in the forefront, while Home and Garden TV channels are dedicated to keeping us in the know. Specialty garden groups—I swear a club exists dedicated to most any plant you could imagine—are numerous and active. And plants are marketed as never before. Boy, are they ever. Branding programs, with Proven Winners being the most widely known, promote plants that someone somehow has deemed the best of the best.

I hear tell that meatloaf and macaroni and cheese have found their way onto the menus of some of the finer restaurants around town. Certainly a case of what is old is new again. Not surprisingly, the same thing happens with plants that fell from favor decades ago, which in recent years have risen again to reclaim their popularity. Hydrangeas are a prime example. They've been around for years, but who until lately has given them much thought, let alone garden space? Now we see dozens of "new and improved" hydrangea varieties clamoring for attention. Tree peonies, very fashionable and desirable in grandmother's garden, are back with a vengeance after a hiatus in the late twentieth century. Succulents, fancy leaf begonias, heirloom vegetables, and flowering shrubs all sported a checkered past but are now hot, hot, hot. I wouldn't venture a guess at what's next.

The grand old lake estates, whose entrances were often marked with catchy names—Cedarhurst, Cedar Shores, Chimo, Gobbins Farm, Green Trees, Highcroft, Little Orchard, Locust Hills, Northome, Squirrel Haunt, and Walden—are a memory. We don't live that way anymore. No more cutting gardens large enough to supply the neighborhood with flowers, no more greenhouses to store tropical plants through the winter, no more terraced formal gardens highlighting the broad vista from house to lake, no more of anything that requires the labors of a staff that lived on the property and was on call twenty-four hours a day. So, yes, the kind of work we do these days is definitely reflected in the way people live. I do miss some of the elegance.

It seems we're faced with a greater roster of bugs and blights than Rod and Bill were subject to. Then again, we've also got a greater arsenal of chemicals at our fingertips to combat those bugs and blights—chemicals, one hopes, that are safer and gentler on the environment than the DDTs of old.

The business of Kelley & Kelley really has been a family affair, with four generations of Kelleys (and many of their spouses as well) taking their turn in one capacity or another. Bill died in 1978 at age 85; Rod, 88, in 1984; both pretty much working almost to the end, to some degree. Retirement never seemed a likely option. Later generations of Kelleys that people the payroll include Bill's son Bruce in the surveying department and Lloyd's son Les, who operated the landscape division for many years until his death in 1992, at which time I took over at the helm.

Of course the business has prospered over the span of a hundred years because of the dedication of hundreds of employees, too numerous to mention individually. Hardly a summer passes these days that a former employee doesn't stop by to say hi and reminisce a bit about work "back then." The memories we recall are usually pleasant, but perhaps those are the only ones we choose to remember. It is to those employees, past and present, and to the thousands of customers who have provided the motivation to keep us inspired, that the company owes its success and longevity.

Working with Les

C elebrating ninety years of plants in 2012 gave me a dandy excuse to reflect on those years past, mainly on the importance of the customers, employees, and vendors who have provided the incentive to keep us moving ever forward with exuberance and delight. For me, the occasion served to bring to mind memories of working with the Kelleys, specifically Dad. I thank Arla for suggesting I put a few of these memories on paper.

For Les Kelley, I don't think there was any question about whether he would join the family firm. In the late 1930s, he attended the University of Minnesota's Ag Campus (as it was called then), and learned a lot in the field from Uncles Bill and Rod as well.

I, on the other hand, never felt a career at Kelley & Kelley was preordained. Perhaps because I was so close to it for so many years, early on I didn't see horticulture as a career option. That changed in the spring of 1971 when, after success in finding a job in journalism eluded me, I bit on Dad's suggestion to spend the summer at K&K, the idea being that I would take up the journalism job hunt again in the fall. Needless to say, fall never came for me; ever since that summer I've been firmly entrenched in plants.

My recollections of the business extend back to the mid-1950s at least. For as long as I can remember, Dad

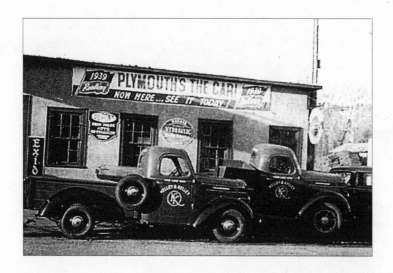

came home for lunch during the work week. Mom always had something tasty cooked up, certainly something better than a lunchbox would hold. Quite beside the opportunity of a home-cooked meal, Dad had (I can say this now that he's gone) a favorite soap opera airing over the noon hour that for years and years he wouldn't think of missing. Something sappy, I'm sure—something I hardly thought a grown man would be consumed with. At any rate, nearly every day at noon Dad would return home driving a truck. One that particularly fascinated me as a little kid was a vintage dump truck, whose box was hoisted, if I recall correctly, by some sort of wheel that you turned. (Nowadays they're all hydraulic, of course.) I delighted time and again in trying my hand at hoisting the box and was disappointed if this wasn't the truck that Dad drove home. (I might mention as an aside that as an adult I never adopted this habit of breaking the work day by returning home for lunch. Alas, I have neither a doting wife at home over the noon hour to whip up a delectable meal nor a fascination with soap operas.)

Back to the 1950s. After lunch, Dad would some-times ask if I wanted to tag along as he made his after-noon rounds of the jobs where his crews were working. I didn't have to be asked twice. Haven't kids forever loved riding in trucks? And I always enjoyed seeing the fine estates. But to me land-scaping work looked like nothing but just that—work. No labor-saving devices back then.

Les circa 1943

It's hard for some of us youngsters to recall a time when fresh produce wasn't available year 'round in the grocery stores, but so it was in the 50s and 60s. In win-ter during that era, bibb lettuce was grown in the K&K greenhouse, and as much as could be grown was sold to the classy Waytonka Market in Wayzata and to the local country clubs. Dad often had me come in after school to help harvest, and wash and package lettuce for delivery early the following morning.

Winter conventions of the Minnesota Nursery Association must have been held during a break from school, because I remember as a grade-schooler ac-companying Dad on several occasions. The gatherings were held at the old Leamington Hotel downtown. Oh boy, was that a treat. As kids, we rarely got to go downtown and certainly never had experienced what a hotel was all about. I felt pretty grown up as Dad introduced me to his cohorts, and I felt pretty proud of him, as he seemed to know everybody and to be friendly with so many of his peers. That was a side of Dad I'd never experienced before.

Another pleasant diversion was visiting local nurseries with Dad. K&K at one time grew plenty of its own trees and shrubs, perennials and annuals. But numerous nearby nurseries provided stock as well, and we often stopped by on our circuit to see what was being grown or to place an order. Close by down Watertown Road were the Butterfields, George and Vi, who had banks of greenhouses stepping down the hillside chock full of plants. While Dad tended to plant business I had fun exploring.

I never had a real job at the nursery as a kid—not one that paid money, at any rate. But I was called upon now and again to help out. Puttery little jobs they were. The summer of 1963, however, brought a task I have to admit sounded like real work. The greenhouse, built in 1937, was in need of refreshing. The framework of redwood, supposedly one of earth's long-lasting woods, wasn't proving so. My part in the rebuilding task was to wash the panes of glass as they were removed, all 1056 of them. (No, I hadn't committed that number to memory; I just now went out to count them.) I don't recall why washing the glass was necessary; rain does a fairly good job of it. We haven't washed those panes since.

Summers during college Dad got me a job with the caretaking crew on the Lucian Strong property here in Orono. Even though K&K had a long association with the Strongs, I don't think the job was offered as a favor, nor was it make-work designed to help send a teenager through college. No, I got a good taste those summers of just what goes into a landscape maintenance day.

Ed Moen, the long-time caretaker, and his wife Bette, lived on the property. Ed was a real pro—dedicated and conscientious. I learned to be dedicated and conscientious, too. If the day dawned rainy, I was expected to call Ed to see if there was work. There usually was; a favorite rainy-day job was polishing the brass doorknobs throughout the house. Perfection was demanded and expected in any task. Don't turn that six-foot-wide Toro riding lawnmower too sharply or you might end up with an uprooted lawn, and an upbraiding from Ed. Keep water off the tuberous begonia leaves or spotting will result. Walk softly across the Har-Tru tennis court. Scrub tools at the end of the day before putting them away where they belong. I learned to drive a tractor and how to wash a car properly. It was a grand education, and I enjoyed it. I liked the diversity of the work, I liked being outdoors, I liked the people, and I liked seeing the results of a day's labor.

"I liked the diversity of the work, I liked being outdoors, I liked the people, and I liked seeing the results of a day's labor."

But still and all, I didn't let two summers of being a chief assistant to a head caretaker divert me from my career path. It took a weak job market in the early 1970s to do that.

I worked closely with Dad and his crews that first summer and got a good feel for the business, learning an awful lot. But the boss didn't cut his son any slack. I dug holes, I hoed weeds, I hauled brick and loaded trucks. I shoveled gravel and pushed wheelbarrows up hills on sweltering days. I helped unload semitrailers of supplies that arrived well after hours. But you know, despite all the drudgery, after that first summer I was sold on K&K. To me it seemed an obvious conclusion: I liked the diversity of the work, I liked being outdoors, I liked the people, and I liked seeing the results of a day's labor. I never accused Dad of harboring a motive in pulling strings to get me the Lucian Strong job, but in retrospect I consider myself a fortunate kid that he went to bat for me at that time in my life. Lord knows how I would have lasted in the journalism sphere had I landed there.

So, if the boss's son wasn't exactly treated with kid gloves, still the idea that I just might be the first representative of the next generation to come on board did work a bit in my favor. Both Dad and Rod quickly saw that my interest in the company was sincere. They took me under their wings and over time made up for the education I never had.

Dad taught me how to dig trees and to plant them, how to run various and sundry machines, how to sharpen tools, how to load a truck efficiently, how to sow grass seed, how to read a bag of fertilizer, how to plant tomatoes, and how to construct a compost pile. On and on. At some point the boss felt I knew enough to lead one of his crews myself. If you can remember your reaction to that annoyingly young-looking kid they sent to service your water heater or refinish your wood floors or clean your carpets—does he really know what he's doing?—you've got some idea of the reaction I evoked from landscaping clients when I first showed up at the helm of a crew to plant that row of arborvitaes or install that rock mulch. It was a tough sell at times, proving myself.

Dad's crews sunk their teeth into the big landscape

jobs, the wall and patio construction work, the from-the-ground-up jobs. He personally favored the challenge of getting that huge shade tree moved into a tight spot and planted, or muscling that boulder into position just so. I played along for a while, but eventually found my inclination was towards work of a more, should we say, delicate nature. I seemed more suited to garden design and planting, waiting on customers at the nursery, trimming shrubs and small trees—I loved climbing around in small trees—propagating annuals and perennials, and maintaining crops in the greenhouse. Those became the kinds of jobs that filled my days.

Soon our paths weren't crossing so much during the work day. But we still maintained a spot of time at the beginning and the end of the day to compare notes. In the morning, it was mostly business. We took an hour or so before work began to plot the work schedule five days out, sometimes haggling over trucks, equipment, and crews for the day. Now and again we took phone calls from sick employees, necessitating an impromptu juggling of crew assignments. If we had time, we made a quick jaunt through the nursery, noting tasks we'd like the garden center crew to accomplish that day.

At day's end, no matter how busy the schedule, we enjoyed sitting under the locust tree on the front terrace and chatting about where the day had taken us or where the next one would, about how the customer's dog had unearthed the tulip bulbs as fast as we could plant them, or sharing laughs over clients' peculiarities. Oh yes, there were more than a few of those, alright. I can share similar thoughts with any number of fellow employees these days, but it doesn't seem the same as

40

those daily conversations with Les Kelley. Of the times we had during the more than twenty years we worked alongside each other, I most miss that laughter and those smiles, as we shared the joy in a work we both found so dearly rewarding. Isn't that rare?

Partners

Mostly, Arla and I are pretty agreeable. We have similar taste in music and interior decoration, fashion and politics, food and travel. We both like fires in the fireplace, winter walks in the woods, and summer parties in the garden. We're lucky that way. I can't say that it was these shared interests that drew us to each other in the first place. Rather, these compatibilities revealed themselves later in our courtship. You'd be correct in assuming it was plants that were the matchmaker. Again, lucky. We can count a few couples in our sphere who share a delight in gardening, but we think it's a pretty rare happenstance.

Gardenwise, I'd say Arla and I have developed, across our twenty-plus years of joint planting, weeding, and deadheading, a devoted partnership to the point where we can't imagine gardening solo. When we're puttering in the garden we're not always side by side; still, we share both a sensitivity and a trust. Though Arla might ask what I think about moving that floppy salvia or doing away with that artemisia suffering with the summer muggs, she knows I'd agree with most anything she has in mind. And I'm sure she'd reciprocate the feeling if I asked about reducing that patch of ajuga along the path in the western garden or removing the lower branches of the birch clumps so that the lawnmower guy (me) doesn't continually graze his scalp during his weekly rounds. For a married couple who are both avid gardeners we're amazingly on the same wavelength.

I must admit it wasn't always thus. In our early days together I suspect we were both used to being single and making our own decisions, not needing to ask permission from anybody for anything. A collaborative venture can quicklv slide off the rails if the parties stomp away in a huff and refuse to speak to each other for the rest of the day on account of a disagreement over whether to deadhead the Siberian iris. What good is that? I do recall a few tense moments over what we soon came to realize were inconsequential trifles. Did it really matter if the pathway entered the garden at point A or ten feet to the north of point A? Did it really matter if the boxwoods were planted in a straight row as opposed to a staggered one? In the grand scheme of things such concerns shouldn't be concerns at all. Why quibble?

There are other matters that don't need sanction. Arla is in charge of planting and arranging the collection of pots displayed on the back terrace. She does a swell job and has much fun with it. If I joined in I'd only be muddling the works. For me, I take delight in trimming our menagerie of shrubs and small trees, tasks that don't require Board Approval. Other than the projects that go along quickly with two working together, such as spreading compost or cutting down the garden in spring or dividing that long row of day-lilies along Watertown Road, Arla and I generally spend time working at opposite ends of the garden. We don't usually discuss the plan for the day. Over the years we've developed a routine—a loose routine. Actually, we don't talk a lot, we just dig in. I take amusement in edging the gardens, setting stepping stones, and keeping the birdbaths fresh. Arla finds pleasure in filling holes in the garden with recent acquisitions, creating pleasing plant combinations, and keeping plant labels up to date. We both tackle weeding and cultivating. When we set out on a sunny summer Saturday with the goal of tidying up the front garden, isn't it a relief to know it's the two of us together?

"In our early days together I suspect we were both used to being single and making our own decisions, not needing to ask permission from anybody for anything."

The task isn't half as daunting then, and it's always surprising how speedily the job is accomplished. Before we know it the place is in tip-top condition. (Only a slight exaggeration.)

Even though we work at opposite quadrants of the yard, we love nothing more than sharing garden delights—something that wouldn't happen if one partner was off golfing or fishing or biking with buddies while the other was home puttering in the garden. Here's how it happens. I'll be under the white pine removing errant clover from the sweet woodruff. Arla will be seventy-five feet away planting epimediums under the oak tree. I spot a little cluster of leatherwood seedlings. It's a curious enough happenstance that I think Arla would enjoy seeing it. A yoo-hoo from me is a signal to Arla that she should lay down her trowel and come for a look-see. A tree frog nestled in a leaf, a hummingbird at the salvia, or a wild rose blooming for the first time ever, all are bits that we'd want to share. We know we're fortunate to have those occasions.

We might think that two gardeners in one household is pretty darn swell but we're not sure passersby share that feeling. Our landscape is not only fairly visible, but it's also different enough from others in the neighborhood to rate a glance from folks walking or biking along the road. Sometimes it's a thumbs up, other times it's rolled eyes and a shake of the head, as if to say, "Those poor folks, all they do is garden." We always get a chuckle out of the observations from serious bikers as they zip by. We can hear them long before they come into view, youngish men and women at the peak of fitness who spend money on the latest bikes and outfits the way Arla and I spend money on the latest plants. And, yes, we always lift our eyes from our work. Seeing those athletes breaks up the day and reinforces our choice of pleasure over their choice of pleasure.

We recognize our good fortune, putting off 'til tomorrow any thoughts of a twosome becoming a onesome. Would our garden become a lonesome place for one alone? Funny, we don't think those thoughts when marveling at that tree frog or wild rose, or when relaxing on the back terrace at day's end, smiling at each other over what we've created and appreciating the reward of a life spent together just as we've wanted.

Why We Garden

One winter, when we were batting around ideas for the coming issue of *In the Garden*, Arla suggested, "Why we garden."

"What do you mean, why we garden?" said I. "We don't need a reason to garden, we just...garden. Like the mechanic who repairs our vehicles or the vet who sees to our pet's health. It's the way they make their living. We all love what we do, isn't that reason enough?"

"Oh, no, no, no. There's more to gardening than making a living," said she. "It goes much deeper than that." *Well*, I reflected, *if that's the case this notion requires a bit of thought.*

To begin with, perhaps the key is to separate what the gardener does to alter the landscape—designing, planting, maintaining—from what the garden provides in return. The mechanic isn't necessarily defined by what he does—tightening lug nuts and adjusting carburetors—but by the satisfaction he gets in knowing he's helped to keep his clients safe on the road. The veterinarian isn't only about giving shots and diagnosing hairballs, but about the satisfaction she gets in keeping an animal healthy. What is the gardener's satisfaction?

The garden defines a sense of place, it tells us we're home. The garden is steadfast in welcoming us home, no matter what. In that regard, the garden suggests stability and a permanence which is especially gratifying in un-settled, fast-paced times. We're secure in the landscape of home. And it's our home—no one else's. We've made it so. There's a great emotional rush upon driving up the driveway of home. This is where we belong.

Though we've seen the garden day in and day out, if we look deeper, look beyond the collection of plants to a broader memory of nature, the garden reveals itself anew every day. We're new every day. Yes, our garden is specific to its place, its here and now, but also on some subconscious level it reminds us of all the landscapes we've shared in the past. The memory of nature that our garden evokes for me might be of the meandering stream behind our house near which I, as a kid grow-ing up, spent countless lazy summer hours, dreaming of faraway streams, rivers, and large bodies of water. In my mind I floated down that stream, under bridges, around islands out to a wide, open, endless sea. Or my memory of nature might be of Northwoods summers. Effortless-ly, even today, I can taste the pucker-inducing choke-cherry plucked from woodland thickets, I can smell the fresh, warm, Vicks-like scent of white pine needles un-derfoot, I can see the thousand shards of the moon scat-tered across gently rippling nighttime lakes.

Our present-day garden stands in for these satis-fying memories and more—the gardens of a lifetime. Those gardens and I, we've grown up together and grown together, defining a great continuity through my years, like the rings of a tree.

The garden also allows for a sense of a job well done. There's a satisfaction for you. Of course the gar-den is a lot of work, who would deny it. Muscle-tugging, sweat-provoking, blister-encouraging work. But, oh my, look back at the end of a day of fussing over the aconitums and anemones, the echinaceas and eupatoriums, and there's not a feeling of fulfillment that can compare. When the garden is nearing just the degree of perfection we've envisioned, our reward is the satisfaction of having brought this vision of unrivaled beauty to life.

We love to garden because we love to learn. Sometimes the lessons are hard won. From a friend, a savvy gardener, we received a seed-grown hepatica that had deep blue flowers in its bloodlines. We planted it in a favorable and prominent position under the white pine out west. It was a cute little thing. We lived with it (it with us?) for three years before it came into bloom last spring. We watched four buds swell and then burst forth with the most mouth-watering, sky-blue flowers. We were transfixed. Bringing visiting friends out to the prize the very next day, we were crestfallen at a scene of destruction. All four buds had been nipped off. We learned the hard way the value of a wire cage. Disappointments? The practical gardener allows for them. We are students of the garden, that great teacher.

"It's fitting that gardening teaches us to dream. Though the garden is rooted in the present (pun intended), dreams of what could be paint pleasant pictures, keeping us forever moving forward."

Yes, I appreciate the lessons learned while gardening. Simple ones like regarding, with reverence, time and its close relative, patience. There's no use in trying to hurry things along—just relax and enjoy the show. Often times that's a hard one to accept.

Doggone it, with the Garden Club visiting next month, don't we wish the block of prairie dropseed we'd planted last fall was more mature-looking by now? And why does it take three years to develop a mossy patina on those glaringly new-looking stepping stones? And we knew that sooner or later a new house or two would be going up in the field next door; why didn't we plant evergreens years ago? We take consolation in the fact that a little impatience is in the nature of things.

It's fitting that gardening teaches us to dream. Though the garden is rooted in the present (pun intended), dreams of what could be paint pleasant pictures, keeping us forever moving forward. Those dreams motivate us to get out of bed in the morning. We dream of retirement and what those years might offer the garden, we dream of the wondrous day we finally figure out how to outwit the deer, and we dream along with the nursery catalogs, devising great wish lists and planning road trips to favored plant suppliers. Dreams, hopes, possibilities. The garden keeps us everlastingly grabbing more from our days.

We long ago came to the understanding that gardening is not a sport, the participants going head to head with Mother Nature or fellow gardeners. No, the garden teaches us the opposite: that we're not required to keep up with the Joneses. We can *be* the Joneses, setting our own agenda. Gardening isn't about a citation in the Guinness Book for collecting the most and the best. It's natural to long for one more of this or that, but not because we're trying to one-up our gardening friends.

Why do we garden? Perhaps, on the most basic level, it's on account of the wonderment of it all. Who

on earth can help but be amazed at the patch of daffodils emerging in spring and blooming right on schedule after enduring months of icebox-cold soil? Who can
help but be amazed at the intricate flower of the common columbine or the perfect simplicity of the Japanese
anemone? Who can help but be amazed at the sight of
the tiny hummingbird performing for its dinner at the
salvia within our reach? We're not leaving behind any
progeny—not human ones anyway—but we suspect the
plants we've surrounded ourselves with have, in their
own way, been as well-loved for the delight they bring
us daily. That's why we garden.

Early Spring

Neither Arla nor I excelled at winter sports in our childhood, and haven't changed our stripes any with age. So we're content to enjoy winter at arm's length, usually in front of the fireplace, catching up on the previous summer's reading. Even walks with the dog in January are generally anticipated more by the dog than by his housemates.

By the time buds start to swell in April we've developed quite an appetite for dirt, fresh air, and sun on the cheeks. We look upon the little routines of spring with almost child-like glee, maybe because they're such mindless tasks, or perhaps it's because returning the hoses to their assigned spigots from winter storage on the garage wall or cleaning out the bluebird houses are such unequivocal heralds of spring.

Whereas spring eases gradually and unannounced into summer, and summer into fall, not so with the division between winter and spring. One day in April we wake up, walk out the door, wiggle our noses in the air, and know, just know, that this day winter is past, meaning we can begin to indulge in all the rituals that endear us to the home grounds.

Initially, time can be well spent merely standing and looking at the garden, envisioning changes and improvements. It'll soon be time for that winter dreaming to become reality and for space to be found for all those mail-order plants that will be fast arriving. There's all manner of "Oh, look at that" vignettes to see and experience around the yard: tiny mouse nests at the edge of the field, comfy grass-lined depressions in the ground used by rabbits through the winter, snaky little mole tunnels across the lawn, and bits of fluff or a scattering of feathers indicating an incident of some sort.

Then, day by day, dormant plants burst forth in shades of green we haven't seen since last spring. On especially sunny days, sap starts to drip from wounds on maple and birch trees. In the woods, the first elderberry leaves begin slowly to spiral open. The first fern fronds unfold, the first color appears on the wild plum back by the barn. Firsts galore. An exciting time, each day new with joy, even though we've experienced the same joys 30-40-50 springs in a row.

In the midst of all this exploring, spring work commences. Only it's not really work. Nothing too strenuous, and not for hours at a spell. We just kind of ease into it. Sweep a winter's worth of grit and grime off the garage floor—a job that creates great dusty, billowy plumes across the sunlight streaming in the open doors. While in the garage, make sense of the jumble of

tools that weren't properly stowed away last fall. Toss out the odd lots of bamboo stakes and the scraps of twine wrapped around scraps of wood and the tangled-beyond-repair bird netting—all things we expected, I suppose, to make use of someday.

All of this exploring and spring cleaning is also a way to bide our time until we can get into the garden in earnest.

When the garden is dry enough to walk across without damage—not that we haven't been itching to get into it before this—all sorts of tasks await. Perennial foliage and seedheads left standing over winter are removed. This includes the grasses throughout the garden, which floated above winter snow, giving us great pleasure, as well as seedheads of hosta, astilbe, turtlehead, sedum, cone-flower, Russian sage, and Siberian iris. Removing the previous year's foliage on the perennials that emerge very early in spring is imperative. Epimedium, helleborus, and foamflower fall into this category. You've got quite a mess on your hands if tender new epimedium shoots peep up through the tattered mat of last year's leaves. We've learned that lesson the hard way.

"In spring there's no rush, we can take time to remove a few branches, step back to assess and admire progress, and continue."

This is also the time for some light raking to remove the debris that has accumulated since fall—sticks, leaves, and paper that came in on the wind. It gives the mulch a fresh appearance, and emerging bulbs and perennials look all the nicer against newly scuffled soil.

As we're cleaning things up we also do the spring shrub pruning. Hardy shrub roses benefit by a yearly thinning, so we remove older branches that have lost their vigor, as well as any branches that have broken or been damaged by winter vagaries. A gentle shaping to remove wayward branches or to keep the shrub in bounds is appropriate in early spring, especially on shrubs that are not spring bloomers. In this category would fall dogwoods, hydrangeas, clethera, euonymus, ninebark, sumacs, arctic willow, alder, wisteria, and certain viburnums and spireas. Like most garden work, such pruning gives us great pleasure. In spring there's no rush, we can take time to remove a few branches, step back to assess and admire progress, and continue. What a great delight in seeing a tidy garden.

Yearly, we admonish customers against planting perennials too late in the season, yet more often than not we ignore our own advice. And, who knows, maybe our customers do too. Invariably, there's a plant or two that didn't have a firm hold on the earth in the fall. If these perennials are left high and dry after winter, early spring is the time to gently but firmly press them back down to ground level. Of course we could have avoided this frost heaving in the first place by covering susceptible plants with a good layer of hay after fall's first frost.

We're constantly amazed at the tenacity of weeds. Doesn't it seem as though nearly every spare waking daylight moment last summer was spent pulling weeds? Wouldn't you expect, then, a weed-free garden in the spring? Wherever did those mature dandelions, patches of creeping Charlie, and carpets of chickweed come from? Fat and perky and green, surely they couldn't have eluded our hoes last year. Maybe they were just specks last fall and grew undisturbed under the snow all winter? It's a mystery that won't likely be solved, nor need it be.

While we're pondering this puzzle, we reach for the weeding tools and make quick work of the invaders. Weeds pull easily when the ground is moist and fluffy in early spring. We've amassed quite a collection of weeding instruments over the years, yet it seems we reach for the same one or two weeders consistently. Arla grabs her favorite and I mine. They both work equally well, I'm sure, but human nature deems that a plain old trowel is most effective on Arla's weeds and a little sharp-edged, short-handled hook works best in my hand. If my tool is misplaced (horrors!) I'd rather find something else to do than weed with a trowel, and I suspect Arla holds the same viewpoint regarding my weeder.

Some of the perennials in our gardens are notorious space grabbers. Not invasive, plants, mind you, like lysimachia, some campanulas, ferns, grasses, and exotic groundcovers, which can be truly scary in their ability to reach out and gobble up their garden mates. Any plant that the catalog writers describe as ambitious or vigorous is usually suspect and best avoided unless you have acreage to cover up. The plants I'm thinking about aren't the kind that send out roots underground for miles and end up emerging on the neighbor's side of the fence. Rather, these are plants like monarda, Solomon's seal, Joe Pye weed, macleaya, obedient plant, and lamb's ears that spread a bit more rapidly than, say, daylilies or phlox. Early spring is the ideal time to keep these types of plants in check. In our garden, most of them need attention every year if we're to avoid any garden wars. Just as new growth commences and the plant's outer reaches are obvious, it's quite easy with a spade to slice straight down through the plant and re- move the fresh shoots all around the perimeter, leaving a nice chunk in the center. Eventually, of course, this central portion will lose its vigor, and you'll want to replace it with some of these fresh, young shoots.

Each and every year in October when we have bulbs on our minds, we vow to fertilize tulips and daffodils in our garden at the proper time, which is just as they're pok- ing through the earth in the spring. The Dutch claim the fruitful life of bulbs can be extended with yearly doses of nourishment, and who's to dispute this notion. The stars haven't been in our favor in April, so our bulbs have yet to benefit from any largess on our part. The only reason we can use to explain such a lapse is that we never have the fertilizer on hand when we need it. And that's the key to smooth sailing in garden work: having the essentials at the ready. Perhaps a pre-spring task worth tackling would be to take inventory of garden supply needs and make a timely trip to the store. Few things are more frustrating than having to interrupt work to rush out and buy this or that just so you can continue moving ahead, so progress can continue. Alas, we're rarely so organized.

Early spring work doesn't have the urgency about it that summer tasks do. Isn't that one of the beauties of spring—we've got lots to enjoy outside and can while away hours puttering, looking, and breathing deep breaths without fear of falling too far behind in main- tenance chores? Best not to laze away too many hours, though, since spring days do eventually become sum- mer days.

Ah, Inspiration

By this stage in our lives, we're well aware of the elements of garden design, know all about contrasting textures and complementary colors, about balance, and about the importance of light and shadow. We tell ourselves we know it all, but somehow we still have trouble finding inspiration, without which the myriad rules at our fingertips will get us nowhere at all. Most of us weren't born gardeners, and as Midwesterners, we haven't been infused with the tradition of great gardens. There aren't many gardens hereabouts, sad to say, that have been passed down through the generations. Even avid gardeners didn't usually develop that fervor until their first acreage faced them. The question is: How do we develop an understanding and an appreciation for the possibilities before us?

We can subscribe to gardening magazines and collect files of pretty pictures, we can visit gardens far and wide, and we can attend lectures given by noted thinkers. We can do all we possibly can to become learned and still walk away with puzzled looks on our faces. To understand the notion of combining plants of distinctive textures is one thing; to be able to make that idea work for us in the garden is quite another. What exactly *is* the process of working the miracle that results in a delightful garden, one that matches the pictures in our minds? How to coax realization from concept?

To develop that delightful garden, one must first of all know and love plants. Without a keen knowledge of all aspects of a plant's habit, only possession of a heaping dose of good luck and the proverbial green thumb will allow one to successfully integrate that plant into the garden. Several examples from real life—my own—illustrate the importance of knowledge.

Several years ago, Euphorbia 'Chameleon' was all the rage in the plant world. Plants that very quickly become all the rage in the plant world are often welcomed blindly even by keen gardeners. This euphorbia was, indeed, an unusual plant as well as attractive in habit, height, and color. It fit nicely and effectively into our scheme of things. Only after living with this plant for a few years did we come to realize the truth about this 'Chameleon': it was a terrible self-seeder, as bad as any weed we knew, and quickly attempted to take over its neighborhood in the garden. It got the boot—and how—but we're still pulling out seedlings. Had we any inkling of this plant's bad manners, I doubt we would have given it space in the garden or the time of day.

The case of Athyrium 'Ghost', a dandy new fern resulting from crosses between Japanese painted fern and lady fern, ended on a happier note, but did produce some head scratching along the way. For some reason, we'd assumed that this little 'Ghost' fern would be the same height as the Japanese painted fern, which for us is 8 to 12 inches. That proved to be the case the first year we had 'Ghost' in the garden, and we were extremely pleased with this very silvery fern. The following summer, however, we were shocked to see 'Ghost' close to two feet tall! It was still beautiful, but all of a sudden it was in the wrong spot in the garden. Referring to the literature (which we should have done initially, of course) would have told us that 'Ghost' can grow to three feet tall—closer in height to lady than Japanese painted. This miscalculation necessitated a bit of transplanting—which happens a lot around home, anyway—that we might have easily avoided.

Actually, I believe we enjoy the process of gardening as much as the results. What, after all, is the satisfaction in thinking that the garden is complete and there is nothing whatsoever left to do but relax and enjoy its beauty?

For me, a thorough knowledge of plants is a beginning in garden design, and does help to spur on creativity. To reach closer to inspiration, though, what's needed is the ability to "see." By that I mean thinking about and analyzing what is seen, not just looking without registering a response. Mere observation can be fleeting; what is required is a thorough feeling for the rightness of a plant or a plant combination. A handy device to use in developing an ability to see is to make a quick sketch—and one certainly doesn't have to be an artist—of a plant. By seeing the plant clearly enough to put it on paper, I find that I understand its various aspects more fully. It helps me see the texture and substance, learn the form and habit of the plant, the color of the flowers and foliage, the weight, the structure, and the character of the plant. Having all this information in mind, and knowing the style we want expressed in the garden—heavily structured, completely informal, or something somewhere in between—allows me to begin dreaming and to make some sense out of the land at my disposal and of the plants I cherish. That's what shows through in a truly inspired design—the owner's deep love of plants. Isn't it that love, that sympathy, which spells the difference between merely having a garden and being a gardener?

Too many of us, myself certainly included on occasion, are guilty of not taking the time to understand everything there is to know about a plant, and to "see" how it works together with other plants. For example, a heuchera, a pulmonaria, a tiarella, a small-leaved hosta, and a lady's mantle—beloved plants all, but similar in character. To use them all close together in the border would be a mistake, as there would be a lack of contrast in height or shape, in form or texture. It is contrast that seizes our interest and keeps our eyes roaming through the garden. While each of these plants may provide interest in detail, which is one of the things I appreciate in the garden, I also want to see the garden as a splendid composition of a great variety of plants. Let our inspiration in the venture toward a delightful garden be a certain playfulness. Every gardener has the same world of plants at his or her disposal, after all. A distinguished garden results from the ability and willingness to arrange these plants in a fresh manner. If all the gardeners in the world are combining hostas with ferns and Solomon's seal, the truly inspired gardener comes up with an original idea. Why not, for instance, try a wood-land grass instead of the ferns, or a rodgersia in place of the hosta? If all the gardeners in the world have latched onto Angelica gigas, why not do them one better by planting a dozen of them instead of the more usual two or three? Yes, I love looking through garden magazines, but I'm not looking because I want to replicate what I see there. I may snitch an idea or two, but mostly I savor the articles as a tonic for my own creativity. And I think creativity and inspiration are closely related.

Pulling these rambling thoughts together, why not think of inspiration as the feeling resulting from an ap-preciation of and sensitivity for the site, the plants, and the elements of good design? We all have had moments when the stars are in alignment and the corner of the garden we've been laboring over at long last comes together. When the composition elicits responses of "Wow" we know inspiration has struck.

Gardening with
the Senses

We wouldn't garden if we didn't enjoy it. We'd be out fishing instead or sitting on the porch watching someone else garden. For me, one of the delights of gardening is the quiet time it provides. And heaven knows, that's a precious commodity these days, as connected as we are to the whole wide world. Why do we feel it's ever more important to keep in constant touch? I'm still amazed at the great number of people running around all wired up. I generally have more than my fill of being "in touch" with people during the day; at home after hours I'm quite ready, thank you, to situate myself in the garden, pull in my horns, and let the rest of humanity buzz by.

During those peaceful times it's so easy to putter along at some mindless but nonetheless rewarding task such as weeding, cultivating, or deadheading and be light years away, deep in thought. For instance, last summer I was tidying up some pulmonarias that had been ransacked by slugs. While touching the coarse, hairy leaves, I got to thinking about how much our senses have to do with gardening. Oh yes, we all associate the sense of smell with the garden, but the senses of sight, sound, taste, and touch come into play as well.

The only way to intimately know the garden is to experience it through *all* the seasons and through *all* the senses. I thought it might be interesting to explore the garden through each of our senses in turn.

First, smell. Could we have a garden without those warmly fragrant roses and the almost cloyingly sweet smell of 'Casa Blanca' lilies or jasmines or hyacinths? And lilacs. Oh my, the unmistakable perfumey fragrance of lilacs brings back so many delightful memories. The scent of rosemary, artemisia, newly mown grass, sweet peas, and well-rotted compost all pull up images that immediately place us in the yard and garden. And in the fall, the biting, pungent smell of smoke reminds us of the garden of years ago, long before we got wise about recycling rather than burning leaves. The sense of smell, more so than any of the other senses, recalls associations with the garden.

And sight has a no less compelling claim to our attention. It is convenient to break down what we see into color and form, both of which are affected by the quality of light. Colors that are loud and boisterous under a blazing July sun fade and become muted by moonlight. Likewise, in low light, form is reduced to its simplest, losing details of texture and scale.

The appearance of the garden also depends on the seasonal quality of light. Isn't spring sunlight the very best—tentative and delicate, not at all imposing. Greens whisper under sunlight filtered through a canopy of emerging foliage. Summer—oh dear—at times we can't escape its harsh pounding light which drains the garden of all subtlety. Oranges, yellows, and reds clamor for our eye. The faded light of fall begins to glance at a sharp angle across the landscape. A somber light, as through onion skins. Like fall's weather, fall's light can vacillate between cool and warm. Fog hangs over the lowlands where bare willow branches float in a dry ice cloud, while blue-skied, radiant sunlight cascading through buttery ginkgo leaves squeezes out some of the last warmth of the season. Winter's light can be a blinding white or a dull, mean gray. In January, lengthening shadows are cast against diamond-dusted snow, and sunshine bounding around twigs sprinkled with hoar frost brings an iciness to the nostrils. Frost and snow define shapes that in summer are defined by color.

So often our seeing is casual, perfunctory, narrow, limited mostly to assessing colors and color combinations. To look beyond the obvious is to open the possibility to so much more enjoyment in the garden.

Mostly we go to the garden expecting quiet. Certainly the distracting roar of leaf blowers or motorcycles or chainsaws is not a welcome sound as we're trying to enjoy the garden's beauty. Think, though, of the myriad of sounds that are relaxing, that we retreat to the garden especially to experience. Most of us—yes, yes, I'm guilty, too—don't fully appreciate the sounds of the garden. I don't mean the sounds of birds chirping and flitting about or of water splashing in a pool. These sounds we all know. But what about sounds that may be barely audible or that we normally tune out? The wind, for example, produces sounds ranging from a chilling swoosh of pine boughs to the soft swish of ornamental grasses; from the rattling of dogwood branches to the rustling of fall leaves, which can often create a chorus of sounds in different registers. Birch leaves in summer click and clack in the breeze; aspen leaves sound like tiny cymbals as they flutter. In autumn, winds whip up the fallen leaves in great skittering waves of sound. To me, the rustling sound that leaves make as they're tossed up into long, low mounds at the edge of the garden strike a melancholy chord that helps mark the season. Dried seed pods on honeylocust trees produce a dull, hollow clap as they rattle against each other.

"To look beyond the obvious is to open the possibility to so much more enjoyment in the garden."

Seedheads in the garden also raise a ruckus in the fall. We like to plant snakeroot, angelica, and turtlehead in great groups so as to have plenty of seed pods taking up the chorus. And we often favor ironwood, blue beech or white oak because they retain their leaves through winter. The crisp, brown leaves are visually appealing against a snowy backdrop and winter winds gusting through these leaves create a fittingly icy tinkle, too.

There is a metal vent on the roof of our house that clanks and clatters in the least wind. I always associate this metal-against-metal sound with the movement that this same wind is also producing in the garden, so even though it may sound as though the house is coming to grief, nevertheless I feel pleased for the garden.

Usually, the sounds the gardener makes are not loud, nor are we attuned to them. Nonetheless, I find people-sounds worth listening for, too. We're often too absorbed in work itself to hear the sounds of work with hand tools, which lays down a human beat, a human pace.

I've mentioned in past newsletters a little short-handled cultivator inherited from Uncle Rod. I like it a lot. It gets me down on all fours, is easy on the back, and makes picking up weeds a snap. The sound this tool makes as it works along varies with the season, depending on the moisture in the soil. Midsummer is the best of all, when it's a firm, slicing sound through dry earth, every now and then clinking against a small stone or shard of pottery. Other pleasant tool-sounds include the sharp, crisp sound of hedge shears, the snip-snip of pruning shears, the airy hissing or pulsing whoosh of garden sprinklers, the rhythmic scritch-scritch of leaf rakes (in my estimation, the old-fashioned bamboo rakes produce a more attractive sound than the new-fangled plastic ones), the sound of hoes against earth, of steel rakes against gravel paths, of handsaws against buckthorn. These are the sounds of work, but also of joy, in the garden. I can't help but smile on hearing any one of these sounds. Together they're a veritable symphony. Listen closely next time you're out in the garden.

The marvelous Toronto Music Garden approaches sound from a different viewpoint. Not only do the plants themselves provide sound, but the design of the garden is inspired by a cello suite by Bach, each of six movements corresponding to a different area of the garden. Swirling walkways, forest groves, formal flower beds, and broad grass steps framing an amphitheater evoke the various characters and moods of the movements. It's a clever, magical, moving, restful, and jazzy garden, all in one. It really does bring sound to life.

Taking advantage of the sense of taste in the garden seems a pretty straightforward exercise, especially if the garden consists of fruits and vegetables. My family always had a large vegetable garden when I was growing up. I didn't much enjoy working in it, but the fruits of Mom and Dad's labor were mighty delicious and not at all hard to appreciate. What can compare to the warm, acid sweetness of tomatoes ripe off the vine or the unmistakable pungency of soft, plump raspberries eaten out of hand.

These days we likely have more to do with herbs and edible flowers than with vegetables and fruit in our home gardens. Not much unusual here: rosemary, thyme, scented geraniums, nasturtiums, violets, and pansies are all familiar edible plants that we love to have close in the garden or in pots. There are also less common edible plants that some might consider weeds. I'll never forget my Aunt Florence Kelley, who was a great one for living off the land. She knew her weeds and supplemented her diet with plants we today take great pains to eradicate: purslane, lamb's quarters, oxalis, cress, and of course dandelion. One can develop a taste for these things. In memory of Aunt Florence, I keep a few weeds in the garden. Daylily roots, fiddleheads, and the emerging shoots of hosta are said to be very tasty, but I've never wanted to sacrifice the plant to find out. I've never been that hungry.

We shouldn't leave wildlife out of this tasting spree. That is, food for the wildlife, not wildlife being made food for us. As you know, there are all sorts of trees and shrubs sporting fruits and nuts that will attract animals. We had more fun last winter tracking the antics of cardinals on black chokeberry bushes back by our garage. Other plants to consider include any of the viburnums, black cherry, crabapple, bittersweet, sumac, and dogwood. If you can get to them before the birds do, fruit of serviceberry, elderberry, chokecherry, and wild grape are quite tasty. I used to be more curious than I am now and would taste anything in the garden that appeared likely to have a flavor. I'd have to say I'm a bit smarter about things but will still occasionally nibble on a leaf if it looks especially succulent or tender. Most often there's nothing more than a green, leafy taste, as one would expect. I have found, however, that the leaves of boxwood, Corydalis lutea, and English ivy are at least not unpleasant in flavor. I've also found that it's best not to be chomping on foliage when guests are in the garden. How does one gracefully dispose of a mouthful of greenery?

I'd be hard pressed to rank the relative importance to the gardener of the five senses. But since it was touch that touched off this little discourse, it must have struck me as pretty high on the list. A gardener's sense of touch kicks in even before entering the garden. On the way to the garden, there's a stop in the garage to pick out tools for the task at hand—perhaps some string to help set an edge, or wooden plant labels, or a piece of burlap to throw debris onto, certainly a shovel or two, and a hose and watering can. Even by name, each piece of equipment conjures up a feel, a texture, a heft. Smooth, sharp, coarse, rubbery. One's memory holds an imprint of both pleasant and unpleasant tactile sensations. We don't need to rub against nettles to know the result, or prick our finger on a thistle or a rose cane. Spades and pruning shears are sharp, rocks and gravel are abrasive, and gas plant can cause skin rash.

Luckily for us, there's more—much more—pleasure than pain in the garden. Most plants invite our hands into the garden. Who can resist the soft, furry leaves of lamb's ears, velvety rose petals, ferny, frothy astilbe plumes, leathery bergenia leaves, steely bark of beech, satiny daylily flowers, on and on. Each plant in the yard and garden has a unique texture that either repels or draws us in and enriches our time in the garden.

People who don't know me very well think I'm a bit touched when they see me running my hands through the piles of well-decomposed manure at the nursery. For me, it's the feeling of good earth, of sturdy roots and of contented plants. Getting my hands in the dirt is always what I look forward to the most in the spring after a few months away from the garden. It's a touch that compares favorably in pleasantness to the touch of resinous rosemary leaves or corky ginkgo bark. It's a touch that brings me back time and again to the garden and thus touts endless cycles of growth and death, action and repose. As we begin to explore the garden as a place of delight for all the senses, we begin to recognize its exceedingly meaningful place in our lives. Gardening in itself affords us great pleasure. Inviting our senses along for the ride can only heighten it.

I Love to Weed

I don't much mind weeding. It goes with the territory. Is there anything to compare to the feeling of accomplishment that comes at seeing a newly cultivated, weed-free garden?

We had a spate of garden visitors last summer, so we were under the gun to keep the place tip-top. In the best of times, we're able to stay ahead of things with a couple of rounds of intensive weeding during the season and a little spot-weeding in between. But wasn't last year something else? In addition to all the other craziness that came with 2021, didn't the weeds outdo themselves! And where did they all come from?

Our property is clean of adult thistles, so why are we faced with baby thistles in the garden every year? Of course, I suspect that once a thistle seed is airborne it could ride the winds all the way from Chicago to the Black Hills and beyond. Why it feels the need to stop off and pester us in Long Lake is a mystery; it could as easily keep right on going. The gardens close to the house don't seem to get too weedy. They've been around for a while and we've been pretty religious over the years, not letting weeds there go to seed.

When we bought the place, the planting beds up against the house were covered with a layer of black plastic under rock mulch. We're not advocates of either of those materials, so they got the heave-ho PDQ. Plastic and landscape fabric have been touted as labor savers by eliminating weeds and conserving moisture. They certainly don't do a very good job of the former. Weeds can and do easily germinate on top of either plastic or fabric, especially if an organic mulch such as shredded bark has been used. Nor, by the way, are we friendly with chemicals to reduce the weed population. The notion of working in soil laden with who knows what isn't very appealing to us. We have applied generous layers of composted manure to the gardens over the years, but not with the intention of getting a grip on weeds. Although annual weeds may be slowed down a bit by a layer of mulch, seeds still lurk below the surface, so they'll get around to us sooner or later. We all know that certain weeds seeds can remain dormant for seventy-five years.

The gardens along the perimeter of the property, on the other hand, are probably havens for weed seeds dropping in from adjacent wild areas and from the Black Hills. Here, the most obnoxious subjects are nettles, thistles, and grasses, along with the less pesky but nonetheless persistent annuals such as chickweed, purslane, foxtail, and knotweed. Oh, and let's not forget garlic mustard, the current scourge to end all scourges.

I love to know the names of the plants I'm eradicating. "Enough of you, you lousy knotweed." "Out you go, you pesky purslane." It makes the interaction more personal and fulfilling when you know your enemy.

Here is our regimen: the gardens are weedless going into winter, and assuming there is no germination during December, January, and February, they're equally weed-free come spring. We seem to be graced with both cool-season and warm-season weeds, meaning that in spring, many of the perennial weeds make themselves known.

> "There's great job security in the weeding business, and it's a job that's either loved or hated."

We consider ourselves lucky, thinking that we'd finally rid the plot of chickweed and purslane. Then June and July bring warm weather along with bounteous crops of those annuals, and more. In spring, garden soil is moist and loose, making removal of deeply rooted dandelions and thistles a snap. Well, a relative snap, anyway. It's most rewarding to pull up every last inch of the dandelion root, or to follow the long, horizontal root of the thistle to its far end, to make sure that those meanies won't resprout. By early June we'll have the garden free of perennial weeds for another year, at least in theory. Isn't there always a root or two lurking below the surface, waiting to irritate us during summer, necessitating all-out warfare with picks and shovels?

The weeds that give us the most grief are the ones that pop up through a dense clump of dianthus or allium, or through a thick mat of creeping veronica. If we were to snag that dandelion or knotweed by its ears when it was just a pup, we might have success in removing it root and all. Generally, though, it's camouflaged and it goes unseen at such a tender young age. By the time it's big enough to be noticed, we find it necessary to dig up the whole kit and caboodle and extricate the bad from the good.

For knocking out perennial weeds, we prefer a stout dandelion digger or trowel or, if we've let things really get out of hand, a spade. The tool is applied deeply and straight down from the crown of the plant and worked back and forth gently, loosening the plant enough to allow the weed to be pulled out in its entirety.

About the time we've declared victory in the skirmish with perennial weeds and dusted off and hung up the dandelion diggers, don't the chickweeds and knotweeds begin to carpet the garden? Even the names of the plants incite disgust. Though they all begin life as mere specks of green, annual weeds have enough in them to annex vast patches of Veronica 'Georgia Blue' if you turn your back on them.

Likely the peskiest annual weed for us has been chickweed, a prostrate tangle of wiry, brittle stems covered with light green, slightly hairy leaves. Small white flowers occur throughout the growing season, resulting in an overwhelming crop of seeds. It won't do to hoe up a patch of chickweed seedlings and leave them, expecting the decapitated fellows to roll over and play dead. No, you've wasted your time. Every last speck of chickweed has to be removed from the garden (and let's not toss the mess in the compost pile) if you expect your labors to be of any lasting value. We usually leave chickweed removal for a day (or two) when we're in the mood for fussiness. I don't know why we labor over chickweed so; we know it'll be around forever. I guess it makes us feel good to see a clean slate, even if an ever-brief clean slate.

There's great job security in the weeding business, and it's a job that's either loved or hated. Me? I'm with Liberty Hyde Bailey, who once wrote: "Weeds are scarcely to be regarded as fundamental difficulties in gardening, but rather as incidents."

Light in the Landscape

In composing a garden, we consider elements of plant form, texture, and color to achieve a pleasing vignette—pretty straightforward stuff and easily understood. I'd like to suggest one other component that bears on effective design but is often overlooked, and that is light—natural light as opposed to the electrical kind. The play of light came to my mind one Saturday last fall when the garden was taking on those typical dusky attributes that come with September. As usual for a Saturday, we could hardly wait to clear away the breakfast dishes and get to work outside. Though there wasn't much that needed doing in the garden—perhaps a bit of deadheading or removing faded foliage—being outside trumped any alternative.

Grasses and hydrangeas abloom and seedheads of Joe Pye weed, ironweed, and meadow rue were highlights of the late-season garden. All interesting enough, though the muted hues were a notable change from the zesty colors of the summer garden just passed and were a herald of the season ahead. A calmness pervaded, evidence of the slowing down that autumn brings with it. But as morning stumbled along and the sun forced itself higher and higher, we noticed the garden taking on a vibrancy we might have missed on busier days earlier in the season. The sun was casting a sidelong glance across the garden, backlighting and illuminating everything within its reach. What had seemed flat and dull in the high, glaring light of midsummer by fall had been

transformed by an aura of radiance. The buttery glow of the soft fall sunlight modified the garden in an amazing manner.

How often do we fail to take into account the effect sunlight and shadows can have on the landscape? Or perhaps we're not attuned to observing light. It's easy enough to be taken with the plants in the garden at the expense of these more subtle effects. For instance, take note of the way sunlight on the rich red leaves of Japanese blood grass sets the plant afire, or how the shadows cast by the intricate leaves of Thalictrum rochebrunianum double the delight provided by this stately perennial. Similarly, sunlight bouncing off glossy leaves or fruit adds a sparkle not seen on an overcast day.

We retreat from the glare of Minnesota's midsummer sun, but should revel in it at all other times of the year, especially so in the early morning and late afternoon when the light is particularly enticing.

Clever plant selection and placement can enhance radiance in the garden. Unfortunately, we can't *always* be in the right spot at the right time to be taken with the effects of sun on garden plants, but when we are, what a delight! Plants that are notably enhanced by the addition of sunlight include gold- or yellow-leaved shrubs and perennials such as Japanese forest grass, Dicentra 'Gold Heart', Iris pallida 'Variegata', and golden mockorange. On the other hand, dark-leaved plants benefit by being seen against sunlight, their color becoming all the more vivid. For instance, take note of Ligularia 'Britt-Marie Crawford', 'Diablo' ninebark, Cimicifuga 'Atropurpurea', or Heuchera 'Regina' at 5 p.m. on a sunny fall day.

Plants with interesting structure or large leaves present fascinating subjects for eye-catching lighting impressions. Site cimicifuga, ferns, grasses, kirenge-shoma, and ornamental rhubarb where sunlight will play against them. The prominent veins of backlit rodgersia leaves appear in contrast to the rest of the leaf, almost as if captured on an x-ray. White flowers are uncommonly stunning bathed with sunlight. The flowers of the Japanese anemones 'Whirlwind' and 'Honorine Jobert' positively glisten, beacon-like, when drenched in sun. Take note of where the September sun falls in the late afternoon garden. An anemone planted at just that spot and radiating in the sunlight will amaze you. I guarantee it.

Our gardens are not static; plants are in constant motion, it seems, to benefit from conditions that will enhance their attractiveness. There's always the chance for improvement. Why not make it a project this year to watch how the sun moves across your yard and garden at various times of the season. Then select and site plants to take advantage of the lighting that only nature can provide. You'll find that it's definitely worth the effort.

In Praise of Mud

Mud, that inevitable result of water on soil, especially clayish soil, is a dreaded phenomenon. Who'd argue with that statement? Just the sound of the word "mud" conjures up visions of horror. Yet this Janus-faced material is never a more welcome sight than first thing in the spring, after the last patches of snow have evaporated from under the venerable white pines and from along the northerly foundations. Mud? Great! That means it'll soon be high time to get back to work in the garden again.

As kids we had great fun sloshing around in the mud along the creek out back, but we learned at an early age that at times consequences came along with having fun. We knew Mom's raised eyebrows and firm grasp on the doorknob would mean a hosing off outside the back door before we were allowed back inside the house. Now, at an older age, we snarl at boots and tools laden with mud that slow work to a maddening crawl. And deer clomping through the early spring garden wreak more havoc than at any other time of the year. Just the sight of them kicking up mud and mangling tender perennials makes their munching on prized plants later in the year seem almost benign. The dog, who hates with a passion having his feet washed, should consider THAT consequence before tromping through the mud—an activity that seems to him such a necessity.

We're savvy enough these days to stay out of the mud—
at least garden mud. The period of mud extends roughly
between the last throes of winter and the arrival of real
spring, with those first expectant buds breaking through
seemingly lifeless soil and spring peepers beginning their
shrill and unmistakable choral tribute to the season. The
eager gardener can scarcely curb his or her enthusiasm,
but understands from experience the need for patience.
You know, there's really not much to do out there anyway,
until the ever warming sunlight and the gloriously lengthening days coax the garden out of its dormancy.

Yes, yes, it's the same story every year. We'd dearly love
to poke around in the garden to discover whether that valued species peony has made it through another tough winter. And isn't it time to think about exhuming that Zone 5
(no fudging there) oak leaf hydrangea we keep alive year to
year only by burying it? I suppose at the very least we could
cut back last year's hellebore foliage? The mud, however,
reminds us that it's much too early to even think about being in the garden. So we await, often without forbearance,
those first few assurances that spring is really upon us—no
turning back.

The period of mud can be a painful time of the year for
the impatient gardener, but it can also be a time to relax and
come to appreciate the slow, methodical unfolding day by
day of yet another beginning.

We know in our hearts that mud is a sometime thing.

Garden Renovation

There's much to do in the garden come spring, a time when we're not exactly looking for additional work. There are the remains of last year's garden to cut down and haul to the compost pile. That's the beginning. We'll also cultivate the garden lightly to freshen up the mulch, assess and attend to any winter damage to trees and shrubs (deer, rabbit, mouse, wind, and ice), trim and thin shrubbery as appropriate, dig and divide overgrown perennials, fertilize emerging spring-flowering bulbs, commence the regimen of spraying the garden against deer browsing, and return hoses, pots and patio furniture from hibernation. Whew! It's definitely full steam ahead in spring. We're positively itching to get out in the soil again.

So in April, why are we contemplating garden rejuvenation as we work along in the north stretch of the western border? Surely that's a tedious task, one that could as easily be put off. Trouble is, we've done just that. Several times. The impetus to redo this slice of garden was the loss, in a storm, of the mammoth and splendid boxelder that had shaded plants in quite an area. It came crashing down, leaving in its wake hardly a plant unscathed. All of a sudden there was sun, a totally alien concept to the astilbe and aruncus, the actaea and aquilegia that called the boxelder their friend.

Plants that at one time flourished beautifully beneath light shade now pleaded for relief. For a year or two after the devastation we pretty much avoided this piece of garden. Sooner or later we knew we would have to take action; we could not forever stand the thought nor the vision of this ragtag scrap of horticultural calamity. Sadly, the garden had been well thought-out, full, and "finished" in our minds. Our long-term plan for our property did not include redoing this bit of our landscape, not at this time. But it was clearly time, a few years post storm, to move ahead, to move on.

For you it needn't take something as dramatic as the loss of a boxelder to set you to thinking about garden renovation. If you've lived with a garden for nine or ten years, seen it flourish and mature, chances are it's high time for a change of scenery. You can recognize the symptoms, I'm sure.

It's never at all hard to break ground for a garden, especially if you know next to nothing about plants. But from the moment the lily or lobelia is planted, the wise gardener gives up all hope of control. A garden exists over time—its greatest nemesis—and is year by year changing and growing. Slowly, imperceptibly, our plants, in bouts of tantrums, turn against us, mocking our efforts to have our way. Trees grow, obliterating sky to all plants below, or they die, limb by limb, a slow painful decline. Shrubs either do too well, jabbing unfriendly jabs at their neighbors, or become weak and brittle with age. Perennials, against all our wishes, don't hang on forever. Given time, even the most well-maintained garden or landscape becomes tired, no longer fresh and vigorous.

The first step in garden renovation is realizing there's a problem. This isn't as easy as it sounds at first blush. As I alluded earlier, problems usually don't appear all at once. Take that hedge of gray dogwood along our western garden. If you know this shrub's habit, you understand that it is a slow but steady spreader, demanding ever more garden space. Not as rambunctious as mint or monarda, but you just know in time something's going to have to give. A savvy garden visitor once pointed out, "You know, that group of daylilies would bloom if it weren't being smothered by the dogwood hedge." Well, yes.

"Slowly, imperceptibly, our plants, in bouts of tantrums, turn against us, mocking our efforts to have our way."

Pinpointing the problem in the garden provides a focus and mandates priorities. Is the source of discontent the hydrangea that's slowly overgrown its bounds, or the iris that's lost its vigor, as they will? Or the dwarf, compact, sturdily upright (that's how "they" said it was supposed to perform) Russian sage that turned out to be anything but? Those are relatively easy problems to solve.

Sometimes the problem has more to do with design. That pairing of the pumpkin-colored coneflower and the rosy sedum didn't turn out to be as attractive as expected. And what were we thinking?! That Joe Pye weed is much too bold for its surroundings. And that tiarella—why, it's become completely overshadowed by the hosta nearby.

Realize you are not going to jump into a garden renovation project on impulse; assess the garden over the seasons. To get to know your garden, to really experience it as a whole, takes time. Deficiencies that come to the fore in October might not have been at all obvious in July. Quite aside from the plants that make up the garden, consider less tangible elements such as the play of light and shadow over the months. Have you taken advantage of those rays of late afternoon sun poking through the oak tree that might highlight especially stunning plants below? Consider the mood you want the garden to portray: restful, inviting, invigorating, sheltering? Do you want the garden to attract wildlife or engulf you with fragrance?

Sometimes the need for garden renovation arises from a situation out of our control—the proliferation of Japanese beetles, for instance. We used to delight in the old-fashioned shrub roses that filled the air with their spicy aroma. We suppose we could have lived with the destruction the beetles wrought, and we did for a few years. But in the end we waved the white flag in defeat. We couldn't stand the ugliness of the critters, let alone the deformed flowers resulting from their voracious appetites. The roses had to go.

Weather sometimes throws the sucker punch. We'd been developing our landscape for more than twenty years before extreme weather necessitated garden revision. Who knew there was a low spot in the northwest corner of the garden? In the summer of 2013, rains came and came and came, and the water stayed and stayed and stayed, leaving a wide swath of very dead plants in that corner. Needless to say, unanticipated garden renovation ensued.

Contemplating
Compost

At home, a trip to the compost pile and back is a fairly straightforward journey not normally holding surprises. The term "compost pile" is too refined a term, I fear, to describe the pile at our place—a dumping ground for a melange of yard and garden debris that we don't by any means manage as a real compost heap. Yet we find it magnificent in its own way, and on occasion we have succeeded in harvesting from it a wheelbarrow or two of what can generously be called compost.

I've seen many compost piles that are really quite attractive and accessible, not hidden from view. Ours, on the other hand, is nothing at all to look at and is reached by a bit of a trek though the garden, past the brush pile, down a trail through a field, and around behind some scrubby crabapple trees that the deer continue to nibble on and scuffle up. You'd be shocked at the amazing amount of fodder for the pile our little plot creates—all manner of stuff cut from the garden, of course, along with weeds, clippings from edging the lawn, cones raked up from under the spruce out front (gosh, there was an abundance of cones this last year!), annuals dumped out of their pots in the fall, and perennials from the garden that have lost favor for one reason or another. Since we heap plant material on our pile without first chopping it up, nor do anything to speed along the composting process, the pile has become a fairly accurate record of our horticultural lives over the past few years. For instance, digging down last summer to come up with a bit of soil to fill several low spots in the garden (everyone should have a compost pile for just such occasions), I came upon a surprisingly intact cache of gourds and squash that served as part of a fall vignette by the front door in 2008. Now that I think about it, it could have been a year on either side of '08, since I recall our creativity suffered a lapse for several years there. Poking further, a big old Boston fern carcass, amazingly recognizable, brings to mind years of its ferny splendor before it began to lose vigor. It held down a shady corner on the rear terrace amongst pots of fuchsias, begonias, and ivy. We've replaced it, but it will be a while before we see such an expansive plant once again.

A layer or two below the fern in the pile, I unearthed several bushel-basket-sized root masses of spodiopogon, the silver frost grass. A tough and indispensable grass for the rear of the garden, where it will reside forever, this grass should be given room to luxuriate. Not that it spreads uncontrollably, no it doesn't, but when it does finally become a larger presence than the garden allows, boy is it a monster to dig out or divide. The dense mass of roots is tough as ropes. A sharp axe and a brawny gardener are required equipment for dealing with this fellow.

A compost pile is a fine place to learn just how enduring some plants can be. When visiting the pile in late fall, my eyes could scarcely believe the unexpected but beautiful sight of a single stalk of monkshood in bloom, rising out of the heap, pretty as you please. Amazingly—and ironically—the plant appeared to be happier for being totally neglected way back in the compost heap than it ever was while under scrupulous care in the garden. As I recall, we tossed him out in the fall of 2007 when we'd had quite enough of his incessant floppiness. Perhaps this is a hint that we should give up on monkshood in the garden in favor of a select spot atop the compost heap. Garden tours to the compost pile to see what's abloom? Well, it definitely rates a consideration, for in addition to the monkshood, the pile sported blooms of poppies, Siberian iris, phlox, and allium, though of course not arranged in any artful order. We could start a nursery ...

The point is that although not every gardener takes the same hands-off approach to composting that do we, a compost pile *can* be quite a record of the owner's horticultural endeavors, a regular garden journal worth musing over. If ever I disappear from gardening chores, Arla knows pretty much where to find me—out at the compost pile, standing around dredging up pleasant garden memories. Now if only the wretched compost heap would cough up the expensive, favorite garden trowel I know was mistakenly dumped there along with a load of garden weeds (you can visualize that scenario, I'm certain), I'd be the happiest gardener on our stretch of Watertown Road.

Secrets of the Garden

A walk through our garden at home might not reveal, to you, anything out of the ordinary—just a collection of plants, mainly hardy perennials, and a shrub or two including leatherwood and bladdernut (too bad its botanical name, Staphylea trifolia, isn't any more attractive than its commonly used moniker). You would see a few garden benches strategically placed, a battle-worn, moss-covered old boulder (but then I guess all boulders are old), and a small hand-hewn granite trough repurposed as a bird bath; an oak here, a grove of white pine over there, and on the fringe, currants, blackberries, and a curious little white-fruited strawberry. You would come upon specimen trees such as Kentucky coffeetree, a horsechestnut, and a shrubby ginkgo. Footing the south-facing foundation of the barn are a row of old-fashioned peonies. A stone pathway winds through it all, and wide patches here and there invite you to pause and take a deeper look.

Most visitors will pause to look deep and see ... what? The cartoonish acanthus bloom? The unusually large acorns on the oak? The small, perfectly globe-shaped fruit on the pear tree? The beautifully cinnamon-covered, peeling bark on the three-flowered maple? Typical observations, all, and we wouldn't expect more than that. But to Arla and me, our little pause (and we're pausing more and more these days) reveals a deeper level of meaning, of seeing beyond the plant or garden artifact itself to a story—a secret recalled from memory. Secrets abound in our garden—more and more all the time. With the thought that sharing these secrets would reveal to the visitor that deeper level of meaning, we've composed this short tale.

Many of our plants come to us in conventional ways, bought through the mail or at garden centers. We love shopping. Many vacation trips include detours to nearby (or at times, not so nearby) nurseries to try our luck. Other folks bring home souvenirs as remembrances of travel. It's plants for us. We enjoy the interaction when meeting dedicated plantspeople. A tradition has been to devote a late-summer weekend, at a time we're more than ready for a break from doing things in the garden, to scouting out the offerings of local garden centers. A real busman's holiday. We never fail to return with plenty of plants aching for permanent homes.

Such plants carry memories.

For instance, there was the time it took us half an hour of back-and-forthing (at least it seemed that long at the time) to reach a nursery which was within our view but on the opposite side of the freeway; and the time we left a bareroot peony under the car seat for two weeks after coming home with it. Why did we think it necessary to hide it under the car seat anyway? Did we think someone would steal it? (At any rate, it survived.)

Then there was the time we were arranging our plant selections in the car ("I'm sure we've got room for one more"), having already paid for them, and had a dickens of a time squeezing them all in. We had the dog along on that trip—what were we thinking?—and wondered for a brief moment who or what would get jettisoned if it came to that. (It didn't.)

On another trip we purchased a plant in Canada— nothing like it back home—that delayed us at customs to the point where we had to scramble to catch our flight homeward. And we'll never forget the time we came to blows (nearly) with another customer over that last rare trollius at a garden center in Pennsylvania. (We got the plant, and survived.) Forevermore whenever we come upon that abused peony or that fought-over trollius in our garden, how can we help cracking a smile as we recall the stories they hold.

The garden abounds with such tales—secrets known, in the main, only to Arla and me. The truly treasured tales, though, are the ones tied to plants given to us by friends. My experience affirms that gardeners are amongst the most generous folks—free with time, advice, and plants. Plants come from friends in several ways. As a gift for the host/hostess instead of a bottle of wine or a tin of homemade cookies, a thoughtful offering might be a chunk off that slow-growing dwarf

maidenhair fern you've babied along for years in your shade garden out back. (However, gardeners know that when visiting a friend's garden it isn't good form to say something to the effect of, "Boy, that's a spectacular hellebore. I've never seen such a deep, dusky maroon flower, and such a huge, well-grown clump, you must be proud of it." That's well- known gardener's code for "Why don't you give me a piece of that plant next time you're dividing it, and it does need dividing. Soon.")

Sometimes plants come to us almost accidentally. On more than one occasion over the years, while plant shopping, a fellow shopper would lean in (and this tells you how friendly gardeners can be) to assess the plants we've picked out and remark, "I think you'd love this little campanula here. I've grown it for years and wouldn't be without it." We're generally happy for the advice, obligingly popping one of the little campanulas into our cart. If we're not, we'll fumble for some excuse, "Oh, I think we've got that one already. Yes, isn't it a dear." Or some such. Not to sound overly cynical, but I now and again wonder if those kinds of folks aren't employees of the nursery.

Mostly friends bring us plants for no reason whatsoever. They've all found special places in our garden and are mostly appreciated for being one-of-a-kind plants, or at the very least are appreciated for the thought involved. More secrets? I'll relate a few.

Although we'll always have a spot in our garden for the likes of epimediums, hellebores, ferns, heucheras, and such, not all plants hold our love through thick and thin. Today we may go overboard for penstemon or salvia or sedum, feeling a great need to collect every one we can get our hands on. Then just as suddenly, and for no perceptible reason, our fervor may cool. So it was with daylilies, I'm sorry to say. A while back, couldn't get enough of them. Went to all the sales put on by the Daylily Society, and all the tours to see daylilies in other gardens. Talked daylilies nonstop during the blooming season.

Oh, we still find room for daylilies, but we don't dream of daylilies anymore, we aren't seeking out daylilies, we don't drive across state lines in July to visit daylily hybridizers. So it was with a gift from a friend, Jane, of 'Sparrow", a small-flowered daylily of delicate proportions. While we no longer seek out such things, it's still a prized possession. It's one of Jane's favorite daylilies, and has become ours as well, and will forever remind us that there may indeed be room for one more daylily.

On the other hand, we're great advocates of leatherwood in the landscape. We've had great success propagating that shrub, and we now have quite a plantation of leatherwood. An estate doesn't require an excess of leatherwoods, however. They're a darling, but leatherwood is leatherwood, after all, and garden space can be better used to show off a diversity of plants, so though we weren't pining for yet another leatherwood, we were touched at the offer and more than happy to accept Martin's gift of another and have found the perfect spot for it. We see it while coming and going every day.

One of the first gifts we received after we moved to this property was a wedding gift from Freda, a cultivator of stunning peonies. On our own, we might not have made peonies tops on our list of must-have plants. But Freda knew that every yard should be graced with a peony or two so she made a gift of some of her prizes—

big, robust, pink doubles, very old-fashioned and fitting our old farmstead. (We did discover peonies in our yard years later, but that's another story. Remind me to tell it to you sometime.) Freda's peonies get better-looking with each passing year. We planted them at the bottom of the hill, against the old barn, where they stand out and can be seen to good advantage from many parts of the yard. We rarely make the effort to cut flowers from the garden, but every spring at peony time a great armful of Freda's peonies make their way inside and we raise a toast to friendship. What a treat.

Some plants come to us as surplus. Jayne was undertaking a major redo of her garden and needed new homes for a patch of epimediums, so she offered to throw some our way. We agreed. Months went by and we'd almost forgot about the transaction. In late summer she was finally ready to dig up the plants and invited us in to pick them up. We put a few empty boxes in the car, but it was painfully clear as we approached Jayne's place that those few boxes were nowhere near sufficient to the task at hand. (Good thing we didn't have the dog along that day.) We knew Jayne's epimedium patch to be rather extensive, but didn't envision our little wagon, full bottom to top. The small area under the white oak we'd prepared for the incoming plants was clearly inadequate. Plan B was quickly devised, and we were able to fill a fair area of bare ground. Jayne will be remembered in a big way for years to come.

Some plants are surplus in quite another way. I suspect many a nursery has had its inception on account of a garden outgrowing its space. Hostas and daylilies and catmint in dire need of dividing? Why, let's pot some up and sell them. *Voila*, another nursery on the block. Rick wasn't about to start a nursery—he's a pretty sane fellow—but he did have an obedient plant that was inching in on its gardenmates, as obedient plants are wont to do. 'Eyeful Tower' is a bit of a departure in obedient plants. It's five feet tall and its flowers are icy lavender, a color you can see from across the garden. Quite a magnificent presence, actually. But it's still an obedient plant, after all. Not everyone's cup of tea. Having known us for years, Rick felt comfortable asking if we wanted a slice of 'Eyeful Tower', knowing we could possibly say "no thanks." And that wouldn't hurt his feelings. I don't think we've ever refused an offer of a gift plant. 'Eyeful Tower' (who names these things, anyway?), not readily available in the trade, has made a splendid addition to the back of our garden, and soon we'll be asking gardening friends if they want a hunk.

It's only a rhetorical question, as we're not there quite yet, but Arla and I have been known to ask each other, in moments when nothing more important is on our minds, "What do you suppose will happen to our garden when we're gone?" We can't think of a soul who might consider our overly-begardened landscape an asset. When we bought the place we were more than happy to have a clean slate upon which to begin our transformation. Seeing what we've done plant-wise, a prospective owner likely won't feel as magnanimous.

Al and Nancy's niche was rock gardening. They made regular botanizing trips out west and had a knack for propagating and growing Alpine plants to perfection. They were in their gardens every day, puttering and preening. But age, like it does, has left them less able to do what they used to do. Wisely thinking of the future, Al and Nancy have been revaluating their gardens, considering new homes for some of their plants. We've been favored with a nice variety of trillium and hepatica, plants that already have stories affixed to them. Now those stories will find additional chapters.

It's important to be able to identify plants in the garden. Of course plants come with names— Peony 'Sarah Bernhardt', Salvia 'May Night', Tiarella 'Spring Symphony'. A plant lacks identity without a name attached. How do you describe it? It's much more convenient to ask the folks at the garden center, "Do you carry the Sarah Bernhardt peony?" than "Do you carry that double, large, dark rose-flowered peony with silver-tipped petals and a soft fragrance?" Be that as it may, when Ben brought us a phlox some years ago, it came with no name. He said it was just a phlox his mom had grown. It's a delicious pink and we're not bothered that it's nameless. We call it Ben's Mom's Phlox and to us it's none the less special.

> "It's much more convenient to ask the folks at the garden center, 'Do you carry the Sarah Bernhardt peony?' than 'Do you carry that double, large, dark rose-flowered peony with silver-tipped petals and a soft fragrance?'"

Sometimes, folks are in search of good homes for good plants. Nan, moving to new digs, had a yellow ladyslipper on her hands. What to do, what to do. Some plants you're comfortable leaving behind. Not so a ladyslipper. Nan felt we might have just the spot for it. Of course we were tickled at the offer and would have loved nothing more than to add a ladyslipper. But at first we demurred. Still, "no" wasn't to be heard. A piece of woods, high shade, evenly moist soil. A dandy site. What started out as a sizeable clump has flourished, becoming more magnificent with age. It really steals the show, hogging all the attention in its domain. Ladyslippers are extra special in their own right; given its provenance, this one all the more so.

A pair of grand white pines mark the southeast corner of the garden. While they weren't gifts to us, they do have a secret to tell. When we first bought the property, we were younger than we are now—quite a bit younger. That spring, we went to work making lists of things we wanted to accomplish outside. Long lists. Lists of work we knew would require an extra set of hands, or two, if we wanted to make any headway. Luckily for us, Arla had a couple of muscular college-aged fellows working for her who were willing assistants. Gosh, we got a lot accomplished in a short time: removed a gravel driveway, set down stepping stones, laid sod, and planted those two white pines. Of all the work they did for us that weekend I think those boys took greatest pride in those pines. They fell all over themselves taking great pains to see that the holes were dug big enough, that the trees were set at the proper depth, were planted straight up and down, and were well-watered. Sometime later we received a note from the mother of one of the boys encouraging us to contact them if we were ever again in the market for tree planters. They were that tickled to have made a lasting contribution to our landscape. Those boys would be proud to see how straight and tall those pines have grown, and whenever we catch the sound of those white pines sighing in the wind we wonder how those boys have grown and matured.

Even rocks can have secrets at our house. What do you suppose gardeners give each other to mark special occasions? Plants certainly would be fitting, but somehow not singular enough. Plants, welcome as they are, come into our lives all the time. Only gardeners would appreciate giving or getting a rock to commemorate a fifth anniversary. Or was it the tenth? I don't remember. It doesn't matter. We love rocks, but finding just the right ones—the ones that look at home in the landscape—is a trick. Siting is also critical if the rock isn't to look as though it was plopped down yesterday or fell off a passing truck. We like to think we've been successful in those regards. This buff-colored piece of limestone is craggy and mossy and now snuggles at the rear of the shade garden under the low-lying branches of a spruce. It will forever be our anniversary rock, distinguishing itself from other rocks on the property that are merely rocks.

The Winter Garden

What a season, the winter of 1995 – 96. We all have our own memories of it, of course, but those of us who were around the Minneapolis area the third week in January will not soon forget the aftermath of an unusual—even for Minnesota—winter storm. At the nursery, rain began falling at 5:30 p.m. on Wednesday the 17th and continued into the night, not stopping till nearly an inch of freezing rain had fallen. Within hours, every twig and branch, every street and power line, was encased in ice thick enough to do plenty of damage. The tops of birch trees and of pyramidal arborvitae were bent down to the ground. Limbs of ash and tree lilac and boxelder and Amur maple were shattered. The ground beneath spruce and pine and maple trees was littered with tiny twigs.

Our power was off for twenty-six hours. A severe wind on Thursday kept us wondering whether or not entire trees were going to topple under the stress. What a mess. After watching it all in horror for a while and worrying about how long the power would be out, we began to relax somewhat and see a bit of beauty in the landscape, and in the animals drawn to it. It made us think that we're missing a bet in not taking greater advantage of the splendors of the winter garden, if you will.

Spring, summer, and fall are each known for distinctive and delightful displays of color, texture, and form. Well, what about winter? Wouldn't it be marvelous fun to have a landscape to enjoy, and for a change not have to worry about weeding, watering, attacking bugs and blights, and chasing the deer toward the next county? Imagine—days of enjoyment without any labor expended.

For this we need to do some plotting and planning. We need to come up with a list of plants that will give us something to ooh and aah over from December through February or so. We tend to focus on evergreens for winter interest. A stately green pyramid is supposedly just the ticket to add life and zest to the winter landscape. Don't you think the heavy, dark visage of spruce and pine create just the opposite effect, cutting off light and producing dense, ominous shadows? We love evergreens in winter, but let's use them to their best advantage—in combination with deciduous plants that will intensify the beauty and grace of each material.

What plants can we use to add life to the winter view? Shrubs and trees exhibiting interesting bark, buds, or silhouettes come immediately to mind. Consider also trees and shrubs that hold their foliage or fruit through the winter. Perennials can add much to the winter scene as well. Most of us are in too much of a rush to get the garden cut down and covered in the fall in anticipation of winter. Why not wait till spring to remove plant material that might add a touch of interest throughout winter? Dried leaves, stems, and seedheads of many perennials provide long shadows against drifts of snow and subtle reminders of summer's bounty.

Now then, in the bark, bud, and silhouette category, the first shrub that comes into focus is redtwig dogwood, that old standby. The best of the best redtwig dogwoods is the variety 'Cardinal', which retains a bright red color all winter. River birch, which is being used more and more instead of paper birch, has a soft, honey-colored bark that offers a warm contrast to the pure white snow. Another favorite is winged euonymous, or burning bush. The snow that often gathers on its corky bark provides a frosting-on-the-cake effect. With age, the burning bush silhouette assumes a broad, umbrella-like shape, spreading its craggy branches in a horizontal fashion, and its small, glossy orange fruit sometimes persists into winter.

Its silver bark may not be a prime reason to select a shrub for landscape use, but in winter, this attribute is a mighty fine asset. Gray dogwood, for instance, has much to recommend it: cool green foliage turning bright yellow in fall, creamy flowers followed by white fruit that birds devour, and a narrow upright habit that makes it suitable for a range of uses. In winter though, it's the steely color of the bark that attracts out attention, standing in bold contrast to a stark white landscape. On bright, sunny days, this effect is especially noteworthy.

Other choices for gray include aronia (chokeberry), amelanchier (serviceberry), magnolia, blue beech, and ironwood. We admire magnolias for winter because their fat, furry buds bring forth in our minds the vision of the color and fragrance these bushes will provide in spring—winter seems hardly so long when we've got dreams of warmth, greenery, and short sleeves in our heads. Blue beech is a small, round tree with smooth gray bark that appears muscular—very distinctive. Dandy as a specimen plant and also performs nicely as an understory planting, it often retains some of its foliage through winter.

A close cousin to blue beech is ironwood, also known as hop hornbeam or just hornbeam. Ironwoods grow to about thirty feet, making them nice ornamental trees. Their slender, spreading branches form a round, open, somewhat irregularly shaped head. New growth is delicate, and the mature tree forms into a mildly contorted outline, giving an almost oriental appearance. Unusual silhouette. It holds its crisp, tan leaves through the winter, rustling in the least breeze.

We doubt we'd recommend a tree or shrub solely because it holds its leaves through winter, but that trait earns points from us as a plant of merit. Winter foliage adds depth, sound, and color, so we shouldn't sneeze at the red, white, pin, and English oaks that retain their crisp brown leaves into winter and spring.

Oh, heavens, is there a bark we *don't* like? Every shrub and tree has some bark quality to recommend it. We haven't even mentioned the craggy Kentucky coffee tree, the golden rain of the weeping willow, the burnished bronze of Amur cherry, the furrowed corky ginkgo, the flaky cinnamon bark of the Scotch pine, or the deeply ridged bark of the oak clan.

Winter fruit and seeds—besides being lovely, of course—attract birds, another aspect of the winter garden. Many varieties of crabapple will hold their fruit until spring, or until consumed by the neighborhood flock. 'Zumi' crabapple trees outside our front door are a yearly stopping point for cedar waxwings heading south and then again on their return trip in the spring. It's a delightful sight and a marvelous means of marking the change of seasons. Other crabs that retain their fruit include 'Red Splendor', 'Donald Wyman', 'Red Jewel', 'Snowdrift', and 'Adams'.

Other plants to consider for winter fruit or seeds include mountain ash, hawthorn, eastern wahoo, ironwood, Kentucky coffee tree, catalpa, serviceberry, highbush cranberry, sumac, and aronia.

It's interesting to note that we've identified several trees as being notable in more than one category. Both ironwood and Kentucky coffee tree rate high marks in our book. They are favorites around here, and get recommended frequently. They're top-rate trees in all regards. There are mature specimens of both in our gardens if you want to see for yourself what all the fuss is about.

Our focus so far has been on fairly obvious stuff— plants we're used to seeing throughout the seasons. If we didn't give equal time to herbaceous perennials, however, we'd be passing up a great opportunity. We've taken to cutting down in the fall just those perennials in our gardens that don't provide winter interest, while saving the plants that afford texture, movement, sound, form, and color amid the snow. Seeing tufts of ornamental grass or seed pods of baptisia in the January landscape is a pleasant reminder that, yes, spring will come and, yes, there is a garden beneath all that snow and ice. Obviously, we need only consider perennials that are going to rise above the snow line. My, doesn't that vary widely from year to year? Last year, for instance, the strawberry-colored seedheads of Allium 'Ozawa', which are only eight inches tall, were left above the snow line for months.

Other plants you might want to leave standing next fall include Achillea 'Coronation Gold', aconitum, astilbe, turtlehead, cimicifuga, echinacea (coneflower seedheads catching hats of snow appear quite jaunty), eupatorium, hosta—it was a January sighting of hosta seedheads peeping through the snow that inspired this article—Siberian iris, rudbeckia, Sedum 'Autumn Joy', thalictrum, and veronicastrum.

"Customers were either scared of grasses—"Aren't they terribly invasive?"—or felt they didn't fit into the landscape well."

By far, though, our favorite perennial to have around in the winter is grass. We think grasses are even more stunning in appearance in winter than in summer. Their warm creamy stalks and leaves arch gracefully, creating delicate shadows across the snow. After the winter's freezing rainstorm I mentioned earlier, clumps of grass reemerged encased in ice, creating fine sculptures that glistened against the sun. Not all ornamental grasses stand up to the rigors of pelting snow and driving wind, however. Varieties that we find especially attractive during the winter months include both big and little bluestem, (which turn delightful shades of rosy copper for winter), switchgrass, feather reed grass, and maiden grass.

For various reasons, grasses took a long time to catch on in a big way here. Customers were either scared of grasses—"Aren't they terribly invasive?"—or they felt they didn't fit into the landscape well. It can be hard to envision a plant we see all around us growing wild in farm fields and ditches as being suitable for a cultivated garden. Grasses do, however, work beautifully together with perennials such as Russian sage, garden phlox, sedum, aster, coneflower, and rudbeckia. Wispy, thin-leaved, green grasses bring grace and color to a garden of bold colors and heavy textures. Stop in this summer to see how grasses add interest, variety, and delight to the garden. We think even the hardened skeptic will be surprised.

Well, we hope this brief summation will give you some ideas to mull over, if you're thinking about ways to enliven the landscape year 'round. With a bit of planning, it's amazing the amount of beauty we can provide ourselves at a time of the year when it means so much.

A Visit from the Tree Guy

If you live amongst trees and are entrusted with their care, you well know that it's less likely to be a single tree guy who comes visiting than an entire platoon. Indeed, three or four beefy sorts generally tag along with the tree guy. Each has a pedigree. One will be savvy in tree climbing (and thus will rate the premier wage), another will work from the ground, trimming what he can reach. One poor soul is relegated to cleanup, and the head honcho (who may come and go during the job) pretty much just points and stuff gets done.

There's something of the mystical attached to trees, something that surpasses discernment. Oak, oak, oak. How is it possible that one oak can be unique unto itself, quite different from the other two oaks even though they were all raised from acorns produced by a single tree? How is it possible that white pines we planted twenty-five years ago now tower above the house?

And consider the memories of a tree—memories of world events it has witnessed, memories of the generations who have felt comfort and protection beneath its branches, and memories of the animals, two-legged and four-legged, who have called its limbs and boles home. Recalling these memories, we have to conclude that trees brush up against the spiritual.

We are reminded that trees are living markers amongst us, marking weather across the seasons: encrusted with snow, frost, and ice in winter, dressed to the nines with pink or white blossoms in spring, buffeted by wind and pelted by rain during the storms of summer, and acting as foils for fall's sun, which theatrically backlights every twig and branch. Common sightings all, but aren't such workaday displays wonderful? They're the gist of our lives.

So the loss of a tree ... Well, only those who have experienced the loss of a tree can understand the sense of that loss.

Both Arla and I knew the old crabapple tree in the garden out west had to go. Yet we'd debated the pros and cons for years. We had to admit that the tree, seen from across the landscape in spring, furnished in its best white frock, was a fantastic sight. Then again, for years we'd put up with the slimy, stinky mess of fallen crabapples in the fall and the swarms of deer they inevitably attract. Then again, it did provide welcome shade. But it was no great shakes of a tree, having been disfigured and diminished by storms. Then again, it did provide welcome shade. But its shallow roots didn't endear the tree to the garden or the gardeners. Oh dear, a teeter-totter of emotions.

The crabapple tree might be standing yet had we not had occasion to call in the tree guy last winter to look after some routine maintenance elsewhere on the property.

A snap decision. The chainsaws roared.

Etiquette

We love garden visitors. We don't garden for ourselves alone. Half the fun is sharing, whether the visitor is new to gardening or can garden circles around us. We used to be intimidated by visits from noted gardeners, garden writers, and landscape architects until we realized that they often had as much to gain from the interaction as we did.

Of course it wasn't as much what was *in* the garden that caused us moments of anxiety, but rather where we stood on the garden maintenance schedule at the moment. We go back and forth. Do visitors have cause to be offended by a weed or two, or should the plants and plant combinations be the center of attention? Certainly we want to see the yard and garden spit-shined at all times and especially so for visitors. But as we age, we've become more relaxed, and hope visitors don't think less of our gardening skills if they spot a bit of imperfection, sharing snide comments behind our backs regarding that touch of chickweed invading the hellebore or that dianthus in need of deadheading. But I'm getting ahead of myself.

Most garden visitors are the model of propriety, and have no desire to make pests of themselves. For them, following the rules of the road is second nature. For those of you who are new to the game or in need of a refresher, however, listen up. Herewith are a few cardinal rules—fudging allowed—to make your visit to our garden a pleasant encounter for all concerned.

First of all, don't just show up. You may embarrass us by spotting that chickweed or that dianthus I mentioned a moment ago. Further, after all, we might be entertaining other visitors or—even worse—we might be in a state of disarray after a hot, steamy day in the garden. We might appear as if we had been pulled sideways through a knothole on such a day. Of course, if you're "in the neighborhood and didn't think you'd mind if I popped in," by all means we'd love to see you.

Rule #2. If you're in a group, huddle up and be quiet or keep your conversation, *sotto voce*, to a minimum during any introductory remarks from your hosts. Bullhorns are not part of our property's inventory.

Rule #3. Dogs are allowed. Children, if they are well-behaved.

Rule #4. Stick to the paths. We cringe at the sight of visitors stepping into the garden to snap a photo or read a plant label. We're more than happy to do the favor and would feel better about things if it was we who stepped on that primula, not you.

Rule #5. Don't filch cuttings surreptitiously. We're not sure what possessed a young lady—a total stranger—to make a stop recently, obviously premeditated, to cut a bouquet of lilacs from the hedge along the road. Our remark that, "We'd gladly have cut some for you if you'd asked," somehow didn't register, and she appeared not one iota contrite.

Rule #6. Along the same lines don't be too coy about asking for a bit of a plant you admire. When I said we love sharing our garden, I meant it literally. No need to beat around the proverbial bush. A direct request will receive a direct answer and if the time is right for digging and there's enough to share, we're delighted to oblige.

Rule #7. By all means, gift plants are welcome. Otherwise, a hearty thank you at visit's end suits us just fine.

Rule #8. Don't ask to use the bathroom. Chances are, if we've been in the yard puttering away in preparation for your visit, it's a safe bet we haven't had occasion to assure a supply of fresh towels and a vase of fresh-cut posies.

Rule #9. Don't overstay your welcome. A tell-tale sign is if we start gazing away in the direction of unfinished garden work or start nervously fingering the Felco pruners in our back pocket.

Rule #10. Reciprocate. Invite us to your garden. We're generally well-behaved, and those busman's holidays are always a splendid change of pace. Or maybe we'll just stop by.

The Green Pot

Do houses have junk drawers anymore? As a kid, I
well remember a drawer in the kitchen between
the sink and refrigerator that had become (by default or
on purpose, I'm not sure) a repository for bits and pieces of anything deemed useful—or not—that didn't seem
to belong anywhere else in the house: a short length of
wire, a fork with a broken tine, a screw of a curious size,
a clutch of keys whose use was long-forgotten, locks
whose keys had been lost, a toothbrush with splayed-
out bristles, eyeglasses that didn't fit the prescription of
anyone in the family, a tiny screwdriver for tightening
the tiny screws in those eyeglasses, and various paper-
clips, pushpins, rubber binders, and a tangle of those
twistems used to cinch bread bags. They all found safe
harbor in the junk drawer. Odds and ends, certainly,
but you'd be surprised how often something or another
in the junk drawer came to the rescue. Need a shim for
shoring up a wobbly table? Check the junk drawer. A
pair of dice? A picture hook? A grease pencil? Check
the junk drawer. Anyone in the family could put stuff
in or take stuff out. There was no jury deciding what
qualified for the junk drawer, but I suspect mostly it was
Mom, tired of shuffling oddments hither and thither.

Perhaps these days we're less frugal, or tidier, or
lacking imagination. Whatever the case may be, we

haven't had a junk drawer for years and, truth to tell, I can't say we miss having one. Arla and I are sort of anti-accumulation; stuff lying around gives us fits. We like surfaces free of clutter. We will admit, however, to having trouble with the trove of reading material that annually gathers, threatening to disrupt our happy life. Some of the stuff gets read and tossed, some gets read and filed, and some gets read, clipped and filed. And some, if we're too busy to deal with it right away, finds a temporary home in a big green pot in a living room corner.

Some years ago, while browsing in a store in Chicago by the name of The Golden Triangle, we came upon a green, classically proportioned, glazed pot of Asian ancestry that we couldn't resist. We bought the charming piece to enjoy in the house, not to be potted with plants and placed on the back terrace. Soon it became a sort of limbo for reading material in need of further sorting. In time it became such an important part of the household that it had to have a name, so we christened it "the Green Pot."

"Arla, where did you put last month's edition of *Fine Gardening*?"

"It's in the Green Pot."

Nursery catalogs arriving midwinter get a quick once-over before finding their way to the Green Pot so we always know where they are. Of course, it may take some digging to find what we want when we want it. That Plant Delights Nursery catalog might by now be sandwiched between layers of all manner of printed material: *Minnesota Monthly* magazines, the Taste section from a newspaper of months ago, the University of Minnesota's alumni magazine, newsletters of various and sundry plant societies, and road maps of midwestern states.

But the Green Pot can hold only so much stuff. Now and again, the pot gets full to the brim. And on some occasions we simply get tired of flipping through the accumulation. If you've ever shopped for Oriental rugs, with the salesperson pulling back rug after heavy rug on a tall pile, hoping against hope you'll sooner than later find your heart's desire, well that's what searching through the Green Pot seems like sometime. At such times, we'll dump it all out and see if we can make sense of it, discarding material we should have gotten rid of long ago and haphazardly organizing the rest.

With its trove of catalogs, I guess you might say the Green Pot is where our plant shopping trips often begin. Its importance in our lives is all out of proportion with its modest stature. It is our modern day equivalent of the 1950s junk drawer.

Leaving Home

Arla and I dearly love to travel. And if we're not traveling, we love to dream about traveling, or read about traveling, or clip articles about traveling. The list of "someday let's go to" destinations grows annually.

The trouble with travel, though, is that it requires leaving home. It's hard enough committing ourselves to an afternoon at a local museum or movie theater; travel with luggage and aboard a plane requires forethought and determination. It's not that we've gotten old and stubborn and eccentric (at least I tell myself that's not the case), but aren't there always convincing arguments in favor of staying put? The idea of a trip may be impressed on our minds months and months in advance of some faraway event—perhaps a convention, a tour, a lecture series, or an open house. The well-honed routine prior to any travel adheres roughly to the following pattern.

Ten months before the event, we receive an invitation to an Arts and Crafts weekend in Asheville, North Carolina. "Hmmm, look at this, wouldn't it be fun?"

Two months later: 'You know, if we were to go to Asheville, we could visit Aunt Dee and Uncle Robert nearby at the same time, and wouldn't the Biltmore Estate be a treat to see at that season of the year as well?"

Another two weeks pass: "If we're going to Asheville, we really should make reservations."

Yet three months later, while reading the Sunday paper: "Hey, here's some dandy airfares to D.C. Why don't we fly there and drive down to Asheville—lots to see along the way."

A month before the event: "If we're going to Asheville, we really should make reservations."

Two weeks after the Arts and Crafts weekend in Asheville: "Well, I guess we're not going to Asheville."

You see, the combination of inertia and the mere thought of the responsibility of being away (and, mainly, the thought of leaving the gardens, even if ever so briefly) has scuttled yet another fun trip. It happens all the time. We can get someone to stay with the animals, we can engage a neighbor to water the potted plants, we can have mail and newspaper delivery suspended, a cousin might mow the lawn or shovel the snow, as the case may be—all this can be neatly and easily arranged, but what about the gardens? We know we could never leave during April-June, when there is so much to do and experience in the garden. Plants will be arriving then from mail-order sources, miniature daffodils we planted the previous fall will be a smash in the western garden, epimediums will be in full, glorious bloom—don't want to miss them. And early spring flowering trees and shrubs will be offering up clouds of color. There's just too much we don't want to miss. Though we've experienced a lifetime of them already, we really would prefer not to pass up springs in Minnesota, no matter how stunning may be the tulips in Holland or the cherry blossoms in D.C.

July through September are garden tour months and months to stay on top of weeding and watering. Oh, the worries we envision if we were to leave town in July: is that neighbor going to be conscientious about watering in our absence, or will we arrive home to find the once-lush arrangement of potted plants on the back terrace languishing from neglect? Impossible, just impossible, to leave at that time.

We COULD justify traveling in October when there's still much of interest and the weather is still pleasant at many of our favorite destinations. And it's not as though we haven't had enough fun with our own gardens by then. They still hold our interest in October, but, let's face it, they have begun to lose a bit of their luster, so that may be the ideal time to plan a getaway, if only for a few days. We have traveled in October without regret, but are lately finding it easy to make excuses for not being away from home at that time as well. Heck, we've made it through to October without suffering exhaustion or nervous breakdowns. Why do we see the need to get away now?

And as for winter travel—I don't know. Used to be, when I didn't have a care, I looked forward eagerly to a month off in midwinter for a car trip to some corner of the U.S. Now, winter seems a time to pull in, relax a bit, do some speaking and some writing. We don't exactly revel in winter here, but we really don't mind it either. Before we know it, the sun is climbing higher in the sky once again and the cycle begins anew.

Ah, home sweet home.

Shopping

A rla and I have never been much for shopping. The offerings in our sock drawers will have
long since become threadbare and our shirt collars woe-
fully out of style before we drag ourselves off on a shopping excursion. Painful. We are saps for bookstores,
but tend to get lost in the travel section when we came
for cooking. Even worse is when, dazzled by shelf after
shelf of books, we forget altogether what we came in
for. Dangerous. Don't even get us started on Christmas
present shopping. Arduous.

What is it about trips to garden centers, then, that
makes us weak in the knees? In a pleasant way, that is.
Oh, do I hear you wondering why someone who owns
a nursery needs to shop elsewhere for plants? Well, I
confess it is darn handy having access to a garden center right across from home, but no garden center can
stock every plant known to commerce. And even for a
nurseryman, or especially for a nurseryman, a busman's
holiday now and again is welcome. Specialist nurseries,
almost by definition, will have more depth in specific areas than a general-purpose garden center, and such es-
tablishments always reach out and grab our attention—
more so if they're specializing in something we love
but can't get enough of. We're not slighting mail-order
nurseries. Over the years, we've weeded out the good

115

from the not so good and annually favor a handful of mail-order outfits with our patronage. We always look forward to finding plant-laden boxes on our doorstep in May. But filling out an order blank midwinter, sending it off and then waiting several months for plants to arrive does little to get the gardening juices bubbling. Wading through rows of living plants, making selections, and filling a cart—now, that's excitement.

Of course, come spring we can't get away on shopping sprees during the week, and on weekends we're busy in the garden. Who would think of venturing forth then? We'd love nothing more than to be the first customers in line when our favorite nurseries throw open their doors for business in the spring, but that's out of the question, so we bide our time, hoping there'll still be a nice selection of the things we covet when we find a moment to sneak away in early June.

There are some pretty choice nurseries within a half-day drive that we return to yearly, or twice yearly. Others we visit on a whim, or a recommendation. No matter their scope, offerings, size, or upkeep, all garden centers have something to offer. Even at a rag-tag affair, with trees and shrubs askew and poorly labeled, and benches ill-stocked with run-of-the-mill, sickly-looking product, there's bound to be at least one treasure languishing out back waiting to be rescued. At the other end of the spectrum are slick operations with hundreds of each plant variety on display, nothing out of place, too perfect, too commercial, no chance for exploring and discovering. In between are the garden centers tailored to the connoisseur of fine plants. The layout isn't perfect, more like the operation grew over time in a somewhat unplanned way. The place isn't made for quick in and out; more for rambling around, which gives you the feeling you may come upon some rare find around the next corner. Not row upon row to the horizon, just a broad selection of nicely grown plants of unusual sorts. At any and all of these garden centers you can pretty much tell, upon alighting from your car, what's in store, what's around that corner.

Garden center catalogs are always helpful; leafing through them when they arrive in early winter prepares us, somewhat, for what awaits our visit and gets us excited about plants all over again after months at leisure. But at that it's only a taste, as there will probably be even more to tempt us in the flesh. Anticipating a road trip, we scribble want lists and pencil in tentative trip dates on the calendar. We can hardly wait and are surprised—though we shouldn't be after all these years—at how increasingly giddy we become as the day of our first sojourn approaches.

I always become wistful when shopping for plants; the task inspires feelings of hope and expectation. At some point I stop at the immature ferns, hostas, astilbes or whatever, marveling over the nurturing that they have gotten thus far and envisioning their long life in our garden as they approach their full potential. I am continually affected by such thoughts as if for the first time. The image is satisfying, but it's not a reverie that interrupts my shopping for too long.

Arla likes to bring the pertinent catalog along to the nursery and check off plants on our want list as we find them. Me, I'm more of a free-range kind of guy, picking up whatever I happen to come upon that looks good. Arla and I take separate carts because we travel at different speeds: Arla more deliberate, up and down each aisle in order, while I tend to jump around, heading off to hot spots seemingly willy-nilly, but eventually covering all the bases. As we're shopping, we'll sometimes double back to catch up with each other, breathless with news of spotting a gem we've been looking for for some time. We never question each other's purchases, knowing they'll all eventually find perfect spots in the garden. I've even given up on rolling my eyes at the inevitable collection of dianthus in Arla's cart. And we never quibble about price, both of us knowing full well what goes into growing a plant for sale. If anything, we comment on a price tag that seems unreasonably reasonable.

We have no other hobbies, and we know few other purchases that can provide such long-term joy. Here's to many more years of shopping.

Cycle of Life

I feel a bit sorry for folks who garden primarily for flower color, visiting the garden center at varying times of the season to pick out what's in bloom that day. Not that the gardener's vision shouldn't be the last word, but don't you think there's a lot more to love in the garden than the pink fluff of the astilbe or the rosy ruff of the monarda? There is the cycle of life.

Even in early spring, or perhaps especially at that time, there's much to engage the gardener. My heavens, the first eagerly awaited buds to emerge out of bareness are a wonder. As they weren't there the day before, they never fail to produce a double take. Soon, stems elongate, leaves unfurl, and then subtly change color from fresh, light green to a rich emerald. The plant takes shape, matures, develops flower buds, and blooms. Petals fade, seedheads form, and the garden is splashed with fall color before the cycle of growth takes its final bow for the year. These last three sentences didn't take but ten seconds to read, yet the enchantment foretold therein is spread over a season's worth of watching, expecting, hoping, waiting, and worrying—and between times, poking at the earth while down on hands and knees.

In our book, all these incidents elicit smiles and wonderment that extend well beyond the satisfaction brought on by floral delights. While not denying the bedazzlement of flowers, we find ourselves evermore propelled to consider the season-long pleasure derived from eagerly anticipated transformations. We know full well what comes next, but are continually bewitched by that unfurling fern frond, that perfect hepatica flower, and that dewdrop magnifying the splendor of the hellebore leaf. The garden is an anticipation of growth to come but also a looking back, a remembrance. The garden is forever changing, forever staying the same. The cycles of change draw the gardener in, eliciting warming, childlike observations: "Oh, look at you, you brave little bud. You've returned for another year, more robust than ever. I remember what joy you've brought to the garden and look forward with thanks to the joy you'll bring again." The plant remembers.

I've called myself a gardener for a good two thirds of my life and I'm still forever amazed and enchanted at the garden's revelations. The garden holds no monotony for me as long as the earth continues its spin around the sun.

Inside Looking Out

I'm writing this in January at the nursery, with papers, catalogs, reference books, and snippets of ideas all spread out comfortably on a large table at a generous north-facing window. It's all pretty much a pleasant jumble that makes sense only to me; everyone else gives it a wide berth. A bird feeder is visible outside—an agreeable distraction. Plenty of mature evergreens  nearby provide cover for hardy animals, mostly chickadees, a cardinal or two, and squirrels, who on sunny days skitter about precariously in the trees, high up off the ground, from limb to limb. A well-used deer trail through ample snow cuts across the vista. An impressive old spruce, each branch dusted with newly fallen snow, towers majestically over the scene. Considering the vista with all the coming and going outside the window, it's a wonder I'm able to commit any words to paper.

I'm usually so busy inside in January that I don't allow myself time to admire the winter landscape. There's loveliness there all the same, if I look for it. The season possesses a charm that changes often—much more frequently in the winter than at any other time of the year. One morning the trees may be crusted with brittle hoarfrost, the next a freezing rain may have encased each twig and branch with molten glass.

Surprisingly, I often feel more attuned to the colors of winter than those of the summer garden. January's colors don't shout or beg, but respectfully ask to be considered. Because there are fewer of them, I appreciate the winter colors and can focus in on minor differences. The sky is the palest of blue—never the rich tone of July—or the color of a burnished coin, somewhere between white and silver. A soft, milky-white morning fog gives safe harbor to landmark trees and telephone poles alike, releasing them slowly from the ground up as midday approaches.

In the winter landscape, brown is an important color, and wants more respect than it's allowed in any other season. In winter, brown exhibits a wealth of diversity. The brown of grasses poking through the snow, for instance, can hold a touch of salmon, that of sedum seedheads a bit of maroon, and that of white oak foliage a rich, leathery russet.

The sun, low in the sky, casts long, violet shadows, a delicate substitute for the color of summer's salvias. Delicate, too, is the sun's light splashed across the sky at day's end—barely a blush and fading quickly, forcing us to retreat inside to the warmth of the hearth. Depending on the light, the vibrant greens of winter spruce aren't at all as lively and green as they are in summer, but a somber blue-black that sets the landscape's mood and my mood as well. The spruce's countenance provides a continuity to the scene over the seasons. Solid. Rooted. Imposing.

The landscape in January is scarcely less beautiful than it was five months before, but it does take observant eyes to seek out that beauty. To these eyes, the garden is out there all the same, no matter the snow. A stillness within us that parallels winter's calm allows us to focus on that beauty. I've always maintained that winter's forced hiatus from garden chores is the greatest gift Minnesota has given the gardener. To me, winter here possesses all the joys of summer gardening with none of the attendant aches and cares.

An Illusion

At times when they can't be *in* the garden, gardeners find it difficult to stop thinking about it, dreaming dreams of it. Especially during a Minnesota winter, dreams of what *could* be—that ideal—keep hope before us. Arla and I have found a crisp January evening, a fire in the fireplace, Ella singing Cole Porter in the background, and a couple glasses of port to be ideal for setting ideas for the next season's garden dancing in our heads.

Yes, always the ideal. Whether or not we ever reach that state of perfection isn't the point. On the contrary, we know we'll never arrive at perfection. But isn't that the allure? Patching together long-ago memories of "garden"—the smell of lily-of-the-valley outside Grandmother's back door, the violets colonizing the wild garden, beans in straight rows freshly germinated in the vegetable garden on the other side of the driveway: these and other images contribute to that vision of a perfect garden. And weren't gardens always perfect in our youth? For a second, such memories fuel an illusion that all's well on the home front. The garden is forever an illusion. A dream away.

The Patient Gardener

At a young age most of us, I'm coming to realize, were advised by our parents that the pace of daily life would quicken when we reached a certain age. Oppressively long days in the school room and marvelously long, warm summer days at the beach or in the North Woods would be a memory. I, for one, didn't believe a word of it.

That is, not until I, several years ago, reached that certain age. Now I realize that those admonitions were true, all true. And isn't it particularly cruel that at a time when the body slows down, the time that the body has available to it speeds up. I don't have the energy of my early 60s; the end of the working day seems to come long before the sun goes down. Used to be I could work happily in the garden til my eyes could no longer make out shapes in the evening's fading light. Now those benches we've scattered throughout the garden, and those lawn chairs on the back terrace that heretofore existed primarily for their contribution to the ambiance of the place, make sense and actually get used—to provide relief to tired bones and weary backs.

At the same time, I somehow feel I'm being shortchanged on days. Are there really still thirty days in September, April, June, and November? It can't be. Before we've made our last New Year's resolution, up pops Valentine's Day, followed shortly by Mother's Day; then the 4th of July takes us by surprise, then it's State Fair time, Labor Day, Halloween. And don't I seem to have missed a birthday or two amongst it all? It can't be possible that AARP wants me as a member already.

Winter in Minnesota—that blissful time when days unfold with a steady, measured gait, allowing the furloughed gardener all the time in the world to check off every last task needing attention before yet another spring shows up. Or so it says in the fine print. Foreign (meaning anyone living outside of Horticultural Zone 4) friends constantly and tediously ask, "Whatever is there for a gardener to do during Minnesota's merciless winters?" Golly, winter doesn't hold near enough days to suit me.

Luckily for gardeners, the path of life's horticultural adventures doesn't allow for disillusionment or defeat. Despite what we perceive as time marching relentlessly on, don't we in actuality have all the time in the world? For isn't the gardener blessed with yet another season, another year, another decade to make things right or to await perfection in the landscape? Many more important things in life demand our time and energy than worrying about why that clematis died unexpectedly last winter or why that prized species peony hasn't bloomed in three years. That, to me, is one of the great joys and great gifts of the garden: it demands from the gardener heaping helpings of optimism, patience, and perseverance, all virtues that play into the hectic pace of life our parents warned us about.

As the Gardener Ages

In the past, I've addressed the issue of "as the garden ages" but now that I'm an aging gardener (by the calendar anyway) perhaps "as the gardener ages" merits some discussion. I haven't conducted any research or asked around, so here are some thoughts strictly off the top of my own head.

The first thing to note is that I don't feel any less like gardening, or have less intensity of feeling for the garden, than I did ten months ago or ten years ago. This is confusing because ... well maybe that isn't exactly the right word. Perhaps it's a feeling of surprise that gardening has come to mean so much in my life. For me, at some point the job became so much more than just a life's work. It's really quite consuming, yet I count myself lucky to have fallen into it. And I don't doubt that the baker down the street and the banker on the corner feel the same way about their professions.

Perhaps the idea of a gardener, the purpose or meaning of a gardener, differs between those who garden professionally and those who garden for the simple pleasure of it. Is the former expected to be a little more adventuresome, a little less content with the status quo, a little more prone to rob the food budget in order to finance trips to the garden centers? I suspect so. Not to put too fine a point on it, but for Arla and me the garden continues to consume a great part of our time and thought and energy, ever more so with the passing of time.

In practical terms, with age I sense changes in our garden style. For a gardener starting out with raw space, and not so much as a peony or a poppy in sight, the urge is to fill up the area post haste. There's vigor galore, not enough daylight in the day. The emphasis is less on the composition of the garden than on covering ground. Phlox and daylilies and sedum are plugged in with reckless abandon. There's no thought that deer might never leave the phlox and sedum alone or that the daylilies will soon enough overtake the scant space we've allowed them. Fine tuning can come later, as soon as we've taken to heart the lessons that nature has pounded into our heads and as soon as we've accepted the fact that there's no way of getting around those lessons.

So, after many trips to the nurseries the plot is beautified to our satisfaction. All's fine for several years, but gardeners become restless, as is their wont. Can't you hear us whining: why do we have to give over so much space to these darn Siberian iris? We've done Siberian iris. We've done lamb's ears, we've done shrub roses and yarrows and nepetas. There's got to be life beyond those things. We've always felt ourselves to be the what-the-heck-let's-try-it kind of gardeners. But with age we find the desire to challenge ourselves intensifies.

Aging gardeners are less apt to be content with the garden as it's always been. If the garden does begin to achieve a new and pleasing order, then impatience arises. It's time to find room for one more space to fill with new visions. Always the new. Alas, there does come a time of no more space (although the remaining expanse of lawn will always be fair game) or no more enterprise to plant and maintain more gardens.

As the garden matures, a gardener becomes more concerned with use of space. Had we made wise choices years ago that Austrian pine, six feet tall when planted in 1996, wouldn't reach maturity in our lifetime. However it sure is plenty big already, threatening to eclipse the garden path and not doing any favors to the plants growing beneath it, either. The older, wiser gardener is less likely to let that sort of thing pass. I'm not certain we would have removed that pine five years ago. This year out it goes.

"Aging gardeners are less apt to be content with the garden as it's always been. If the garden does begin to achieve a new and pleasing order, then impatience arises."

Perhaps we were foolish, years back, in not thinking long-term instead of seeking immediate rewards. Wouldn't we have something now had we planted trees and shrubs in 1994 when we first settled the property? We hadn't the vision. Now we're trying to catch up. The aging gardeners are thinking more about what they'll leave, what difference their lives will have made. Time does seem to be speeding along. The maples, ironwoods, magnolias, and oaks we've planted the last few years are a start; the delight they give us as we plot their growth is beyond measure.

As young gardeners, we started out with ambition to match the garden space at hand; we wanted lots of everything, plant wise. But our desire was breadth, not depth. We couldn't limit ourselves to just salvia, shasta daisies, coral bells, and hosta. No, we wanted a few of everything that caught our fancy. Two or three varieties of coral bells of the nicer sorts would do.

Now I'd say we're more particular. We still crave the nicer sorts, but in certain cases two or three varieties won't do. We've gone all agog over epimediums, ferns, hellebores, snowdrops, and toad lilies, and seek depth in those genera. We'll take the time to search out the specialty nurseries that offer broad ranges of these plants and love nothing more than to learn from growers who are as nutty as we are. We've come to know that we're not interested in collecting every last new coneflower or astilbe or coral bell. One baptisia might be enough for us, though as new varieties are introduced, the question remains which one should that be?

We've become less tolerant of plants that misbehave, not allowing them garden space for long. A ruthlessness has set in; a well-worn path to our compost pile vouches for that. A terminally floppy little bluestem called 'The Blues'? Compost. A sedum whose leaves sport corky lesions? Ditto. In the past, we might have chalked such failures up to inexperience. Now we know it's not a matter of dumb luck when our anemonopsis rewards us with command performance-type blooms.

True, the garden now sports a slimmer crop of weeds than years ago, as we've been painstaking in our efforts to keep weeds from going to seed. Still, weeding is taking up proportionately less of our time these days, mainly because we're not so aghast at the sight of a weed or two as once was the case. We well remember spending entire weekends maintaining the garden. Nowadays our joy of being in the garden isn't dampened by thoughts of work, work, work. We still find great delight in puttering, but it's a bit of a surprise to see the garden less demanding of our labor.

One last point worth mentioning. These days, we're apt to be found relaxing on one of those well-placed garden benches that heretofore we'd thought of as mere ornament. We've come to a heightened appreciation of the concept of 'tomorrow.' Puttering in the yard past dusk doesn't hold the allure it once did. There will always be another day. In other words, we're enjoying being in the garden without feeling guilty over not striking a down-on-hands-and-knees pose at all times. And maybe that's the ultimate reward of the growing older gardener—the permission we grant ourselves to act our age.

Contentment

Contentment. I'm not sure I'd given much thought to the idea pre-pandemic. I'd pretty much done as I'd pleased without a notion that life should unfold otherwise. Now, with constraints, we have learned to live with less. Less flying about at the drop of a hat, less socializing with family, friends, and cohorts. (No holiday gatherings? Heavens!) Less time spent in restaurants, theaters, galleries, health clubs, stores, and out and about. (My, how we missed the State Fair.)

Who among us could have conceived that all the narrowing of options would be a relief. Do we need to be constantly on the go? Are we often racing frantically to keep two steps ahead of what life throws at us? That said, could we now take the time to cultivate an appreciation—see anew—the magic close to home? How often we walk down that garden path, peer out that window, or sit on that terrace bench without really seeing, feeling, smelling, touching. These days, time has given us the chance to be at home at home.

Each day is a performance, no two exactly alike, and each one in its own way captivating. In the sense that life is composed of a kaleidoscope of experiences, my life hasn't been especially extraordinary. I certainly couldn't pen an autobiography that would be termed gripping, inspiring or unusual.

I watched the squirrels cross the road. I walked to get the mail. I sat on the back terrace at sunset. Thus, the days pass. These experiences, these memories—the song of my life—are home ground. They're the accounting of my days.

Our world may have contracted in so many ways for the moment, but at the same time it's overflowing with wonderment. No, we don't have to wander off our little plot to be amazed at the best of life—changing cloud formations, patterns of light and shadow, wind in the willows, sounds in the night, the texture of a leaf, the complexity of a seed pod or flower, birds fluttering about the feeder, the fragrance of a late-blooming snakeroot. That's contentment—being at peace where we are, knowing that in being right here, not in Chicago, Seattle, or Venice, we're not missing anything that matters.

Stuff I've Learned
Along the Way

I well remember my life of fifty years ago, a young pup just starting to wiggle my toes, so to speak, in the horticultural waters of the Lake Minnetonka area. I'd grown up with plants all around me but never amassed much practical knowledge and certainly never gave a second thought to making a living with plants. As a pre-teen kid, being conscripted into working summers at the family nursery always seemed to get in the way of things I'd rather have been doing. Despite it all, I learned how to plant beans and corn, loved to mow the lawn and pull weeds (still do) and could deadhead a pot of geraniums with the best of them. Hardly enough breadth of knowledge, though, to pass muster as a well-rounded gardener. But isn't it the way of the world that fifty years later, folks are now asking me how to plant beans and corn. In the early years I suspect I could be accused of pretending to know more than I did. Forgive my immodesty in stating that such accusations would seldom be appropriate nowadays.

My gardening education? I'll admit it was pretty catch-as-catch-can—learning by doing, taking cues from mentors, from reading, traveling and attending lectures. I feel fortunate in having had a circle of folks around me willing to help sharpen my wits—and I still do. I now consider it worthwhile to share what I know liberally with others. I'm flattered again and again by the kind notes I receive from today's young pup gardeners with whom I've exchanged a tip or two. I well understand their feeling of not knowing how to proceed or even how to commence trimming that spirea or dividing that phlox or diagnosing that plant ailment. In any endeavor, there's a great joy in succeeding and in seeing others succeed.

> "Be bold. Do nothing by halves. If you think five is too many, plant seven."

Along those lines, how about a few of Steve Kelley's words to live by, tidbits that fall under the rubric, "Stuff I've learned along the way."

Be open minded. Be prepared to adapt, to reconsider. The inspiration that you need to carry on comes in many forms—don't close your eyes to it. Take a nod from nature, loosen up, be spontaneous.

I'll be the first to admit that I'm not always "with the program" on that one. To wit: Arla will pick up a plant at a garden center and direct a questioning look towards me. I will react to her questioning look with another one: "Do we have a spot for that?" No, you don't have to have a plan for everything. Don't be set in your ways. Study what those you admire have accomplished—no need to reinvent the wheel all the time. There's no shame in taking cues from others. That formal garden at some grand estate might not be your piece of cake, but perhaps you could mine a few ideas just the same—a cunning plant combination that caught your eye, or an insight into plant layering, or an approach to using sculpture in the landscape. Surprise yourself by trying something today that you'd not thought yourself capable of yesterday.

That said, the next tip is: **do your research**. I can't tell you how many plants we've moved or removed because we miscalculated. Too much shade? Whoops; didn't know it couldn't survive that. Trees grow ever taller? Whoops; didn't know that that upright white pine would one day (sooner rather than later at that) tower over our two-story house. We just wanted something modest in height to hide the utility boxes. What a waste of a stunning tree. We're weeping over that loss years later. And, oh my gosh, we could plant a substantial nursery with plants we removed from our landscape because they were, as the catalogs are fond of saying, robust. You well know the ones that from the beginning are intent on trouble with their invasive roots or a proclivity to seed themselves around.

Another tip: **take your time**. Take the long view. There's more fun to be had in gardening if you rid yourself of the thought that tomorrow will never come. Tomorrow always comes, and the next tomorrow, too. What a joy there is in watching things grow. Twenty years later you'll glance back and say, "We planted that—now look."

Patience. It isn't always a gardener's strong suit but it should be. I find myself smiling inwardly as the person behind me in the checkout line rolls his eyes or drums his fingertips against his cart while I write out a check for my purchase. I heard a humorist recently comment that writing checks in checkout lines was allowed only by those over the age of seventy-five. Oh dear, I'm not quite there yet.

Be bold. Do nothing by halves. If you think five is too many, plant seven.

Use strong lines in laying out edges of beds and borders. If it's a straight line, make sure it's as straight as a proverbial arrow. Believe me, the least blip will be ultra-noticeable, like a piece of spinach lodged between your two front teeth. Curves? Make a statement by drawing broad sweeps, not squiggly little lines that insult the land they're drawn on. Better one broad curve than three insignificant ones. Assert your fearlessness.

Consider the view from inside. Plan vistas visible from every window—vistas that are vibrant, no matter the season, lend depth and perspective, and capture the eye and lead it ever onward. A window serves to focus attention, forcing the viewer to look more thoughtfully. Our septic mound at home is in full view, smack dab out the kitchen window above the sink. We had nothing to say about where the mound was put, but we did have a say in what got planted on it. Native grasses now fill that view with beauty and interest.

Choose large pots. I'm much more offended by containers that are out of scale on the small end of things than on the large.

Mourn your losses and move on. Never forget that garden design is, like life itself, a negotiation between love and loss. Every plant's joy in life is to repay your love, which it does many times over during its lifetime. Isn't that enough?

Be bold in your pruning. Several years ago we planted an informal row of dwarf red twigged dogwood for a customer, the purpose of which was to camouflage utilities yet still retain a view of the lake beyond.

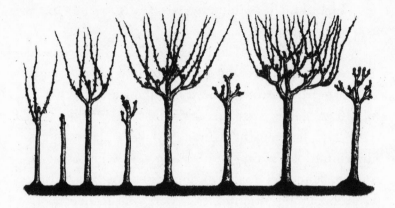

Well, "dwarf" is a relative term, and we knew that some light trimming of the little shavers would be required to maintain the desired effect. Our customer agreed she was up to that task, but several years later she contacted us, asking for help. Indeed! Following years of neglect or timidity with the pruning shears, the dogwoods had crept up to obscure the shore and were inching ever skyward. Although a stellar view of the lake was still possible, some well-timed go-get-'em years earlier would have made the pruning job a lot easier.

The best training in the world for any type of work is to **keep doing it**, day in, season out. Make mistakes, hone abilities, build confidence. Wishing a garden into existence is no easy matter. Nonetheless, don't be afraid. You can succeed if you're prepared to. Dig in. Have fun. You can't muck things up beyond repair. Nature is your ally. Mostly.

The Best of the Best

The opinionated gardener (and isn't that just about all of us?) loves to share whatever comes to mind. An alluring new perennial, a newly discovered garden center, a pest-eradication solution that *really* works, book reviews, gripes, concerns, and gossip all are fair game. In that vein, and in light of K & K's hundredth anniversary, Arla and I concocted the zany idea of sharing our hundred best of the best. The task was more difficult than we imagined, but here goes.

Epimedium. Choose *one*? Love them all, but if forced to pick the poster child for the genus, how about 'Pink Champagne'?

Hosta. Given the annual proliferation of varieties, wouldn't this selection change from year to year? At the moment 'Sunset Grooves' might take top honors. Doesn't the heart just quicken at the sight of those thick, golden, insanely puckered leaves with wide green margins? Distinctive.

Daylily. I'll be the first to admit that many of the new un-daylily-like looking cultivars don't exactly sweep me off my feet. A top looker (and stellar performer) is old reliable 'Hyperion'.

Fern. Why look further? For my money, good old maidenhair fern is strictly top shelf.

Groundcover, Sun. Eschewing for now the usual low sedums and alliums, Thymus albiflorus comes quickly to mind as a dependably hardy creeping thyme. Shiny green leaves and pure white flower spikes May through July.

Groundcover, Shade. This is an obscure little veronica, but it never fails to captivate us and visitors alike. Veronica repens 'Sunshine', at only a quarter-inch tall, is as close to ground-hugging as can be imagined. As its name reflects, 'Sunshine' is known for its gold foliage that slowly increases to a tight mat and tolerates considerable foot traffic.

Bulb. Fritillaria meleagris, checkerboard lily, makes me smile.

Grass. Sporobolus heterolepis 'Tara' (prairie dropseed) is tidy, well behaved and combines nicely with any manner of perennial. A gardener touching his or her toes into grasses couldn't go wrong with this one.

Herb. A split decision. I'd not be without rosemary, but since Arla is the cook in the family, I respect her wish, which is bay laurel.

Tomato. We've tried many over the years. For disease resistance, yield, and flavor 'Mortgage Lifter' is nonpareil.

Clematis. I know the large-flowered types are iconic, but I still reserve space in the garden for that gold standard of small-flowered clematis, Clematis paniculata. Rambunctious. Free-flowering. Tough as nails. Immortal.

Rose. Were it not for Japanese beetles (or whatever the politically correct name for them is), we'd grow the biggest and best roses in the world. And we'd have the old-fashioned, extremely fragrant rugosas—'Frau Dagmar Hastrup', 'Belle Poitevine', and 'Blanc Double de Coubert'. If we could find them.

Hydrangea. In the ever crowded collection of hydrangeas, several stand out. We favor 'Little Lime,' whose creamy flowers edge towards a deep rich rose come fall.

Crabapple. 'Adams' knocks down high marks for disease resistance and persistent fruit.

Dahlia. 'Thomas Edison'. Rich, eight-inch burgundy flowers on a compact plant. Luscious.

Solomon's Seal. The usefulness of members of the genus Polygonatum is well known; we are great proponents of their garden worthiness. They weave themselves effortlessly into any woodland scheme. A particular favorite might be Polygonatum 'Chollipo', a moderately-fast spreader. 'Chollipo' grows a modest (for a Solomon's seal) eighteen inches tall, is adaptable to part sun or shade, and is distinguished by reddish-maroon stems and green-tinted white flowers.

Marginal Perennial. Beesia. With its glossy, bronzy, leathery foliage and summer-long small, white, starry flowers, this five-inch beauty is an absolute knockout—in a quiet way. We've been ones to regard Beesia's Zone 5 hardiness rating with skepticism and have had good luck coaxing it along year after year for some time.

Marginal Shrub. Some sources rate Stewartia pseudocamellia hardy to Zone 4, most only to Zone 5. We've gone out on a limb with this one. With its fragrant, camellia-like flowers in early summer and luscious, salmony fall color, worth the risk.

Native Plant, Sun. Geum triflorum (prairie smoke). Perfectly at home in native plantings and in the garden. In early summer, nodding, reddish flowers give no hint to the wispy, whimsical display of namesake seedheads to come.

Native Plant, Shade. Claytonia virginica (spring beauty). An apt name. Early in the season, spring beauty's charms beguile all comers with its delicate, star-like pinkish flowers on plants only three to four inches tall. Naturalizes delightfully.

Tropical Foliage Plant. Phormium. We love phormiums in pots. Their leathery, sword-like leaves grow in a fan-like clump, and are marked beautifully in shades of salmon, olive, cream, bronze, and rose. Their boldly upright forms contrast pleasantly with the garden's softer, more relaxed outlines.

Tropical Flowering Plant. Only because we have a splendid specimen left to us by a favorite, dearly-departed friend do we nominate gardenia. The association is priceless and the floral fragrance divine.

Fragrant Plant. Doesn't mockorange's come-hither scent just pull you back to Grandmother's time?

Scented Geranium. Scented-leafed geraniums have been a mainstay here for generations. These scratch and sniff plants are a hit with kids of all ages. My favorite variety is peppermint, whose large, wooly leaves are more pepperminty than peppermint itself.

Long-Blooming Plant. Hellebore is a slam-dunk. Nothing comes close.

Early-Blooming Plant. What do you know, hellebore again.

Hellebore. Okay, since we seem fixated on hellebore at the moment, which one ranks tops? Another one of those toughies, but 'Onyx Odyssey' stands out.

Spring Ephemeral. Erythronium (dogtooth violet or trout lily), known as much for its dark green, strap-like fleshy leaves distinctively mottled with purple freckles, as for its winsome, nodding, creamy flowers.

Plant from Grandmother's Garden. A patch of lily of the valley outside the back door made it worth the detour in spring.

Flowers for Cutting. For their long-lasting shelf life, astrantias and Allium 'Ozawa' can't be beat.

Small Tree. Oooh—a toughie. Blue beech, with its year-long interest, might be a contender. So would three-flowered maple with its delicately exfoliating bark and strawberry sorbet-tinted foliage come fall. Couldn't go wrong with either, but the latter might have a slight edge in my mind. Today.

Large Tree. Ginkgo, hands down. Distinctive. Carefree. Appreciate its history.

Tree for Fall Color. Maples and oaks would be obvious choices but I'm going to be a contrarian here and nominate tamarack. Isn't it a surprise when its green needles change their stripes?

Small Shrub. 'Bobo', the tidy little (two to four foot tall) hydrangea is a knockout when abloom—smothered with creamy flowers aging to dusky rose.

Medium Shrub. Viburnum carlesii, growing 6 to 8 feet tall, is an all-around good kid. And if there's a shrub with a more delicious fragrance, let me know.

Tall Shrub. Yet another head-scratcher. We've enjoyed both white fringe tree (Chionanthus virginicus) and seven-son flower (Heptacodium miconioides) for many years. Both measure eight to ten feet tall at maturity. The former shines in spring with spicily fragrant white flowers, the latter in September with clusters of fragrant creamy flowers. Wouldn't be without either of them.

Shrub for Fall Color. I'm not sure Mother's rouge was as luscious as this shrub's fall foliar display, but who cares—both Mom and Viburnum 'Forest Rouge' are winners in my mind.

Winter Interest. Hakonechloa macra (Japanese forest grass). If snowfall is scant, this grass displays clouds of swaying, tawny foliage, capturing the eye like no other. Graceful.

Small Evergreen. Boxwood is so very versatile.

Large Evergreen. We planted a pair of white pines 25 years ago. Lately they are beginning to look mature. Love that soft green needle and horizontal branching.

Invasive Plant. Can we have a favorite pest? Why not. Plant-wise, garlic mustard seems to be the most reviled interloper at the moment.

Invasive Animal. No contest—deer. We regularly see a dozen in a pack and are terrified at the damage they inflict.

Weed, Favorite. If there is such a thing. We'd nominate Pilea pumila (clearweed). Pulls easily and thus, satisfying to eradicate. We can't be mad for long at any weed so obliging.

Weed, Non-Favorite. On the other hand, our nemesis is Stellaria media (common chickweed), which routinely infests any perennial in its vicinity. We get to practice our salty language pulling *this* one out.

Dividing Tool. If precision isn't required, a sharp spade serves just fine. If the plant under consideration is precious and isn't too large or woody, a hefty, sturdy kitchen knife does wonders. Don't spend a lot of money on this one; search garage sales for something that looks beefy.

Hand Pruner. No need to cast your eyes beyond the industry standard—the Swiss-made Felco. Either model #2 or #4. Sturdy. Reliable.

Trowel. We don't mind spending a bit more on tools that we use a lot, and a trowel is in our hands daily. Used to be we sourced (when did it become fashionable to trick nouns into verbs) trowels at leading garden supply companies until their tools became dumbed down. Now, a sturdy, well-built stainless steel model from Brook & Hunter is our heart's desire.

Cultivator. The little hand-held spring-tined cultivator is a marvel.

Saw. The versatile, convenient folding hand saw made by either Felco or ARS fits the bill.

Edging Device. Any old spade will do, of course, but I like the feel of the half-moon-shaped blade of the tool made just for the job. A joy to use.

Small Digger. Those of us of a certain age well remember Smith and Hawken, hawkers of quality gardening stuff. They sold a poacher's spade that had a curved blade, ten inches long by five inches wide—just the perfect size for planting potted perennials or for digging holes in tight spaces.

Hori-Hori Knife. The one and only. A must-have for all manner of gardening tasks.

Dandelion Digger. Can't be beat for capturing every last bit of root, and what's more sigh-inducing than *that*?

Two-Wheeled Device. The classic yard cart—the one with big pneumatic tires and plywood sides/bottom. Lightweight yet sturdy. Arla and I fight over it.

Muck Bucket. Invaluable around the garden. I like the flexible rubbery one—you can grip both handles in one hand. Comes in baby bear, mamma bear, and papa bear sizes. Lightweight. Indestructible.

Stringline. Essential gear for maintaining crisp garden edges. The antique one we inherited years ago has the line attached to a spike on one end and a reel for easy winding and unwinding on the other end. Simple. Fun to use.

Watering Can. Use anything that holds water. Those 2.5-gallon jugs that kitty litter comes in are handy for siphoning water from the rain barrels. Classic and more practical is a Haws two-gallon galvanized can with a long spout, helpful for getting to nooks beyond easy reach.

Sprinkler. We are without a sprinkling system (our choice), so we rely on dragging hoses around the garden (the lawn is on its own) when drought is severe. Our very favorite sprinkler, not only because it's old-fashioned, but also because it covers a large area with a gentle spray, can be pictured, I think, from a description: horizontal U-shaped legs support the thing, from which a vertical pipe comes up three feet, at the top of which are two two-foot arms stretching horizontally with nozzles on either end that whirl around, spraying water over parched plants with a hypnotizing swish-swish sound.

Hose. Don't those hoses that turn themselves into knots test your patience? Nothing worse. We gladly spend a bit more to buy a hose that is flexible and kink-free. A rubber hose, rather than a polyurethane one, seems better able to keep the steam under our collar to a minimum.

Hose Nozzle. Indispensable when you have to use the hose. At the moment, we're favoring a variety that looks and acts like a firefighter's hose nozzle. Easy on and off and everything in between.

Rain Barrel. By the Barrel, an outfit in southern Minnesota, does a great job of converting oak wine barrels into rain barrels. We like the look and they make rainwater smell kind of elegant to boot.

Rain Gauge. A simple copper receptacle holds a stock glass vial. All you need.

Kneeling Pad. Nothing wrong with those spongy ones. I go the natural route and fold up an old burlap bag.

Gardening Gloves. I perform best with bare-naked hands in the garden, but when absolutely required I prefer gloves that are barely there.

Garden Hat. Somehow the ever-popular baseball hat doesn't seem to fit my head, or vice-versa. It always needs fussing over (the hat, not my head) to keep it from going all askew. The bucket hat, while not as stylish perhaps, suits me fine.

Garden Shirt. So why don't I like spending extra on shirts? Simple—I'm hard on them. No sooner are they broken in than I snag a hole in the sleeve or stain the fabric indelibly with sap or paint or who knows what. Instead of Ralph Lauren, then, my golf shirts are strictly Brand X.

Footwear. Despite my age and seniority, I still do a fair amount of work work—digging, clomping around and climbing trees. (Whoops! Our insurance company is not supposed to know that.) So I need a boot that's sturdy. Good old Red Wings can't be beat. In addition to being sturdy, they are light and are comfy for the long haul.

Plant Labels. Oh my gosh, we've tried them all—wood, plastic, tin—with results that didn't wow us. So we had Cousin Chris Kelley fabricate a sturdy aluminum model, 1" by 10". The label itself is printed on a Brother label machine. Professional-looking and long-lasting.

Plant Supports. We appreciate supports that fade into the foliage and thus don't make a big deal of themselves. For us, branches from lilacs or hazelnut work well. Use whatever you have at hand.

Container. None are more valued than those given us by friends.

Gardening Season. Spring. And let me point out at this junction that I couldn't garden in a locale without well-defined seasons. The change of pace each new season brings to Minnesota gardeners is invaluable.

Garden Bench. What is generally considered the Lutyens (Edwin Lutyens, 1869–1944) Bench, has actually been around since the 1600s. It took Lutyens, British architect and garden designer, to popularize it. No matter its provenance, we appreciate this wooden bench for its organic lines, which fit attractively into the landscape.

Steppingstone. The natural, understated, neutral look of New York Bluestone complements the garden nicely.

Compost. The benefits of organic matter in garden soil are innumerable. And, for this purpose, nothing is easier to concoct than compost made from leaves and garden litter.

Reference Book. The most dog-eared book in the garden section of our bookcase is Michael Dirr's *Manual of Woody Landscape Plants*. Invaluable. And, unlike many horticultural reference books, anything but dry.

Notebook. The moleskine product feels good in the hand; if only the thing could be prodded to get its owner to use it.

Gardening Magazine. In its later years, *Garden Design* was beautifully done and offered practical solutions to everyday situations. Equally lavish in its design, the English *Gardens Illustrated* is likely a wee bit less useful for us stateside, but still a good read.

Horticultural Library. Andersen Horticultural Library at the University of Minnesota Landscape Arboretum. A welcoming place.

Mailorder Catalog, Printed. Of course there are fewer and fewer of these, but the one from Digging Dog

Nursery out California way still delights us. Oh, how we miss Dan Hinkley's Heronswood Nursery catalog.

Mailorder Catalog, Online. Far Reaches Nursery, based in Oregon, is admired for its plant selection, quality of plants, and appealing, easy-to-navigate website.

Defunct Plant Source. We still lament the loss of Flower Factory in Wisconsin and Garden Vision in Massachusetts.

Bird in the Garden. Hummingbird, although the elusive bluebird ranks a close second.

Annual to Attract Hummingbirds. Salvia. With their eye-catching color—fuchsia, orange, hot pink, red—and upright habit, these long-blooming, tubular-flowered annuals are irresistible.

Garden Animal. Dog, well behaved.

Critter Repellant. We're troubled by deer mostly, rabbits occasionally. If applied religiously, early spring to late fall, Liquid Fence does the trick. Against slugs, diatomaceous earth seems to have some effect.

Garden Writer, Non-Fiction. Many folks in the know consider Henry Mitchell (1923 – 1993) the best garden writer this country has ever produced. I concur. He loved words and was insightful in his use of them. I return to his essays again and again for inspiration.

Garden Writer, Fiction. Here was the process for compiling these hundred favorites. Arla and I sat down one Sunday afternoon in early January and rattled off whatever categories came to mind. The first sixty were a snap. Then we began to experience "writer's block." Slowly we edged towards seventy-five, even slower toward ninety. The last ten weren't realized until several days later. Then commenced adding the nominees and attendant commentary. That wasn't too difficult, but we came to several categories that gave us fits, so we set them aside for a bit. Over a couple weeks we had them all knocked out, save for one—Garden Writer, Fiction. For the life of us we couldn't come up with a single writer of garden fiction. No amount of brainstorming helped us. We're not sure there is such an animal, so we've left this entry blank, hoping one of you might be more clever than we. Come on, a little audience participation please.

Fictional Garden Character. Amos Pettingill, nom de plume of William B. Harris, founder of White Flower Farm. Amos's lighthearted, witty scribblings were always anticipated.

Public Garden, U.S. Chanticleer in Pennsylvania. Creative and at times quirky, we want to take it home with us.

Public Garden, Foreign. Les Quatre Vents, the garden of Frank Cabot (1925–2011) in Quebec, Canada, known for the sprawling landscape now dedicated to horticultural outreach and education. Open a heart-breakingly meager four days a year. Cabot drew inspiration from around the world; influences included traditions from England, China, Japan, and Italy.

Landscape Architect, Dead. Oh dear. Too many influential designers to choose from, both native and foreign-born. Tapping only one on the shoulder seems a fool's errand. That said, I respect Jens Jensen (1860 – 1951), who was a pioneer in exploiting indigenous vegetation to produce a radically new concept in landscape design. He believed the built landscape should capture the spirit of nature and he advocated for a heightened sense of stewardship toward the environment.

Landscape Architect, Alive. Michael Van Valkenburgh (b. 1951). Not known for a singular style, rather noted for his habit of fitting his designs to the site.

Mentor. I've identified a few in my years, but none as dear as Great Uncle Rod. I doubt I'd have stuck with it without his attentions.

Hybridizer. Brent Horvath. Brent is thoughtful, has chosen out-of-the-ordinary genuses to work with, and is a stickler for painstakingly evaluating his introductions.

Garden Experience. Sharing. We always maintain we don't garden for ourselves alone; we fancy a steady stream of visitors. Keeps us on our toes.

Reason to Start Gardening. There is so much to learn. The gardener is young physically and mentally.

Lessons Learned. Never give up, there's always another year. Don't strive for perfection; a garden's purpose in life is to provide joy, not stress.

Way of Spending the Day Other Than in the Garden. Nursery hopping. Do you doubt it?

Saying. "You should have seen the garden yesterday."

Gardening Partner. My wife.